EXECUTIVE FUNCTIONING SKILLS FOR TEENS: FROM STRESS TO SUCCESS

PROVEN TECHNIQUES TO GET ORGANIZED, CONQUER PROCRASTINATION, STAY FOCUSED, BOOST CONFIDENCE, AND ACHIEVE YOUR GOALS IN SCHOOL AND BEYOND

ALEXANDER GRANT WEALTH

© **Copyright 2024 - All rights reserved.**

The content contained within this book may not be reproduced, duplicated, or transmitted without direct written permission from the author or the publisher.

Under no circumstances will any blame or legal responsibility be held against the publisher or author for any damages, reparation, or monetary loss due to the information contained within this book, either directly or indirectly.

Legal Notice:

This book is copyright-protected. It is only for personal use. You cannot amend, distribute, sell, use, quote, or paraphrase any part of this book's content without the author's or publisher's consent.

Disclaimer Notice:

Please note the information contained within this document is for educational and entertainment purposes only. All effort has been executed to present accurate, up-to-date, reliable, and complete information. No warranties of any kind are declared or implied. Readers acknowledge that the author is not engaged in the rendering of legal, financial, medical, or professional advice. The content within this book has been derived from various sources. Please consult a licensed professional before attempting any techniques outlined in this book.

By reading this document, the reader agrees that under no circumstances is the author responsible for any losses, direct or indirect, that are incurred as a result of the use of the information contained within this document, including, but not limited to, errors, omissions, or inaccuracies.

TABLE OF CONTENTS

Introduction   7

1. UNDERSTANDING EXECUTIVE FUNCTIONING   11
   What Is Executive Functioning? Breaking Down the Basics   11
   The Science Behind Your Brain: How Executive Functions Develop   13
   Executive Functions in Action: Everyday Scenarios   14
   Identifying Your Strengths and Weaknesses in Executive Skills   16
   The Role of Emotions in Executive Functioning   18
   Why Executive Functions Matter: Beyond School and Into Life   20

2. MASTERING TIME MANAGEMENT   23
   Interactive Element: Task Prioritization Exercise   25
   Using Technology to Tame Procrastination   26
   The Pomodoro Technique: Boosting Productivity   27
   Balancing Academics and Extracurriculars with Ease   29
   Weekend Planning: Maximizing Your Free Time   31
   Overcoming Last-Minute Cramming: Planning for Exams   32

3. ORGANIZATIONAL SKILLS FOR SUCCESS   35
   Digital Organization: Managing Files and Notes   35
   Decluttering Your Space: A Step-By-Step Guide   37
   Color Coding and Labeling: Tools for Efficiency   39
   Backpack and Locker Management 101   41
   Creating a Homework Command Center   42
   Syncing Calendars and To-Do Lists for Ultimate Control   43

4. BEATING PROCRASTINATION   47
   Interactive Element: Journaling Prompt   48
   Setting Small Wins: Building Momentum With Mini-Goals   49
   Procrastination Busters: Techniques That Work   51

Accountability Partners: How Friends Can Help You Stay On Track — 53
From Procrastinator to Planner: Transforming Your Approach — 55
Mindful Moments: Using Mindfulness to Combat Delay — 56

5. DEVELOPING DECISION-MAKING SKILLS — 61
Interactive Element: Decision-Making Worksheet — 63
Practicing Safe Decision-Making: Simulations and Scenarios — 63
Trusting Your Gut: When to Listen to Intuition — 65
Learning From Mistakes: Turning Failures Into Learning Opportunities — 67
Peer Influence: Making Decisions Independently — 68
Building Confidence in Your Choices — 70

6. EMOTIONAL REGULATION AND RESILIENCE — 73
Recognizing Emotional Triggers and Responses — 73
Stress-Reduction Techniques for Everyday Life — 75
Building a Resilience Toolkit: Strategies for Bouncing Back — 77
The Power of Self-Compassion: Being Kind to Yourself — 79
Mindfulness Practices for Emotional Balance — 81

7. SETTING AND ACHIEVING GOALS — 85
Interactive Element: SMART Goal Worksheet — 87
Visualizing Success: Creating Vision Boards — 88
Breaking Down Big Goals Into Manageable Steps — 89
Tracking Progress: Using Apps and Tools for Accountability — 91
Celebrating Milestones: The Importance of Reward — 93
Staying Flexible: Adjusting Goals as You Grow — 94

8. BUILDING INDEPENDENCE AND STEPPING INTO ADULTHOOD — 97
Embracing Adulting: Developing Skills for Independence — 97
Harnessing Technology Wisely: Balancing Use and Avoiding Pitfalls — 99
Learning to Ask for Help: Building a Network of Support — 103

Creating a Personal Growth Plan: Mapping Your Future	105
Celebrating Your Journey: Reflecting on Growth and Planning Ahead	107
Conclusion	111
References	115

INTRODUCTION

It's Monday morning, and your backpack is a black hole. Somewhere in its depths are the homework assignments you swore you'd complete and the permission slip your parent needs to sign. You rush to school, feeling the weight of a thousand tasks pressing down on you. Sound familiar? You're not alone. Many teenagers struggle with the chaos of school, extracurricular activities, and personal commitments. But what if I told you there's a way to navigate these challenges more smoothly and confidently?

This book is here to help you do just that. It's your guide to mastering executive functioning skills—the mental processes that help you plan, focus attention, remember instructions, and manage multiple tasks. By improving these skills, you can reduce stress, achieve success, and unlock your full potential in school and beyond. Imagine having the tools to turn chaos into clarity and stress into success!

Executive functioning might sound like a big, fancy term, but it's really about some essential skills that can transform your life. Think of them as your brain's air traffic control system. They help you organize your thoughts, manage your time, make decisions, and regulate your emotions. When you learn to control these aspects, you're not just surviving the day—you're thriving.

So, why are these skills so important today? Think about the challenges you face daily: Whether it's juggling homework, sports, and social life or trying to make decisions about your future, executive functioning skills are your secret weapon. They help you prioritize tasks, stay focused during study sessions, and manage stress when things get overwhelming. Imagine you're trying to balance school with a part-time job and still want some downtime. Strong executive functioning skills make sure you don't drop the ball.

My vision for this book is simple: I want it to excite and motivate you. Each chapter is designed to empower you, giving you the tools to take control of your life. We'll start by identifying what's holding you back and then move on to practical strategies to help you overcome those barriers. By the end of the book, you'll feel more in control and ready to tackle whatever comes your way.

Here's a quick look at what you can expect:

The book is divided into chapters, each focusing on a specific skill like organization, time management, and decision-making. We'll break down each topic with real-life examples and offer strategies you can start using right away. It's like having a roadmap to help you navigate through the maze of teenage life.

Now, a little about me. I'm passionate about helping teenagers like you overcome obstacles. I've spent years working with young people, providing guidance to help them succeed. I want to make this journey as clear and straightforward as possible, offering accurate and easy-to-follow advice.

By the time you finish this book, you'll have a toolkit of skills to improve your organization, manage your time better, and make decisions with confidence. But remember, this isn't just about reading. It's about actively engaging with the material. The more you apply what you learn, the more you'll get out of it!

Think of this book as your journey toward self-improvement and empowerment. It's your opportunity to embrace growth with an open mind. Each step you take brings you closer to becoming the best version of yourself.

Are you ready to take the first step? Dive into this book with the commitment to learn and grow. Embrace the strategies and techniques you'll find here. Your path to mastering executive functioning skills starts now, and I promise it will be worth it. Let's get started!

1

UNDERSTANDING EXECUTIVE FUNCTIONING

Ever wonder why you can focus intensely on a video game but struggle to stay awake during history class? Or why some days you can get your homework done in a flash, while on others, it feels like your brain is full of static? This isn't you being random—it has a lot to do with executive functioning, your brain's personal assistant. Executive functioning helps you plan, organize, and juggle tasks. When it is on point, everything feels manageable. When it's off, well, that's when you feel like you're starring in your own chaotic reality show. This chapter will make sense of it all and show you how to boost these skills so you can thrive in every part of your life.

WHAT IS EXECUTIVE FUNCTIONING? BREAKING DOWN THE BASICS

At its core, executive functioning is a set of mental skills that includes working memory, cognitive flexibility, and inhibitory control. These components are like the gears in a machine, working together to help you manage your life. *Working memory* lets you hold onto information temporarily, like when you're trying to remember a math formula while solving a problem. *Cognitive flexibility* is your ability to switch gears or adapt to new situations, like when your teacher changes the seating arrangement and you need to adjust. Meanwhile, *inhibitory control* is all about self-discipline, like stopping yourself from checking Instagram every five minutes during study hall.

Every day, you use these skills—often without even realizing it. Remember that time you had to memorize the periodic table for your chemistry test? That was working memory in action. What about when your after-school club meeting got canceled, and you had to quickly come up with a new plan for your afternoon? That's cognitive flexibility helping you adapt. And when you resisted the urge to binge-watch a new Netflix series until after your homework was done, that was inhibitory control working its magic. These skills help you handle countless tasks, even when life throws you a curveball.

Executive functioning plays a major role in your daily life, helping you tackle everything from organizing schoolwork to planning social activities. It's what allows you to break down a big project into smaller, manageable tasks, ensuring you don't end up pulling an all-nighter. Likewise, it aids you in planning a fun weekend with friends, ensuring you've coordinated rides, snacks, and who's bringing what to the sleepover. When these skills are sharp, they make the difference between feeling overwhelmed and knowing you're in control.

But why stop at school and social life? The skills you develop now lay the groundwork for future success, whether you're applying to college or preparing for your first job. Being able to manage your time effectively, adapt to new situations, and maintain focus will be invaluable as you navigate the complexities of adult life. Think of these skills as tools you'll carry with you, shaping not only how you succeed academically but also how you handle the ups and downs of life beyond the classroom.

THE SCIENCE BEHIND YOUR BRAIN: HOW EXECUTIVE FUNCTIONS DEVELOP

Imagine your brain as a bustling city, with roads and highways that represent the pathways of your thoughts. The *prefrontal cortex*, the area right behind your forehead, is the city's control center, directing all the traffic. It's responsible for managing executive functions, like a conductor leading a symphony. As a teenager, your brain is still building and refining these roads, deciding which routes to develop and which to let gather dust. This process, known as *synaptic pruning*, strengthens the pathways you use most frequently, much like a city widening its busiest streets. As you practice specific skills, like playing an instrument or solving algebraic equations, these neural pathways become more efficient. This is *neuroplasticity*, the brain's remarkable ability to adapt and reorganize itself throughout your life.

The development of your brain isn't a one-size-fits-all journey. Each person's experience is unique, influenced by a mix of genetics and the environment. Some of you might find that growing up in a supportive family—where curiosity is encouraged and mistakes are seen as learning opportunities—helps your executive functions flourish. Others might notice how educational experiences—like engaging teachers or challenging projects—significantly shape your cognitive skills. These factors can affect how and when different aspects of your brain mature. So, while some of you may be quick to adapt to change, others might excel at maintaining focus amid distractions.

These changes in brain development significantly impact your behavior and decision-making. As your prefrontal cortex continues to mature, you might notice an improvement in your problem-solving abilities. Maybe you're finding it easier to tackle complex math problems or create a plan for a group project. Similarly, your capacity for emotional regulation grows. You start to manage feelings like frustration or anxiety more effectively, which allows you to navigate the emotional roller coaster of teenage life with greater ease. It's like having a better grip on the steering wheel as you navigate the sometimes bumpy roads of adolescence.

But there's more to consider: Because brain development varies from teen to teen, not everyone arrives at these milestones at the same time. You might have a friend who seems incredibly organized while another struggles to remember their locker combination. These differences are perfectly normal and reflect how diverse our brain development can be. The important thing is to recognize that your brain is rewiring itself for both the present moment and the future. It's preparing you for adult responsibilities, from managing your time effectively to making significant life decisions.

To make this idea more tangible, imagine a real-life situation: You're at school, and your teacher suddenly announces a pop quiz. Panic might be your first reaction. But as your brain develops, you become better at handling surprises. Your ability to calm down, assess what you know, and use your time wisely during the quiz improves. This is your executive function at work, guiding you through the challenges of school and life. As you continue to grow, these skills will become even more refined, helping you not only survive but thrive in an ever-changing world.

EXECUTIVE FUNCTIONS IN ACTION: EVERYDAY SCENARIOS

Now, I want you to picture this: It's the first day of a new group project in your history class. Everyone's buzzing with ideas, but chaos quickly takes over. This is where executive functions really step in. Imagine using your skills to help organize the group: You start by dividing the project into sections, assigning roles based on each member's strengths. Maybe one person loves research, while another is a whiz at creating presentations. By defining clear tasks and setting deadlines, you help your group move from a jumble of thoughts to a well-oiled machine. This organized approach gets the project done—and it makes everyone feel valued and heard, reducing stress and improving the outcome. In this scenario, executive functioning turns a potentially overwhelming situation into an opportunity to shine.

Let's shift gears to the weekend. You and your friends want to plan an epic outing. But coordinating everyone's schedules, finding a ride, and picking a place to hang out can feel like solving a puzzle. Here, executive functioning helps again. You prioritize what needs to be done first—maybe it's getting a ride. Next, you organize a group chat to decide on a location. You talk about options, considering everyone's input and finding a middle ground that makes everyone happy. When unexpected changes arise, like a friend canceling at the last minute, your cognitive flexibility allows you to quickly adapt and find alternatives, ensuring the day goes smoothly. This proactive planning not only makes the outing successful but also strengthens friendships, as everyone appreciates your seamless organization.

Executive functions also shine in problem-solving by breaking down tasks into bite-sized pieces. Suppose you're buried under a mountain of assignments, from English essays to math problems. Instead of panicking, you use prioritization to tackle one thing at a time. You might start with the subjects that are due the soonest or the ones you find most challenging. By creating a detailed schedule, you assign specific times for each task and make sure nothing gets left behind. This approach teaches you to organize your study sessions effectively, allowing for focused, productive work without feeling overwhelmed.

Emotional regulation is another crucial aspect of executive functioning. Imagine facing peer pressure to skip class for a party. It's tempting, but your ability to regulate emotions helps you weigh the consequences. You calm your initial anxiety and think through the situation logically, deciding to join your friends later instead. Have you ever had a disagreement with a friend? Instead of reacting impulsively, pause, reflect on your feelings, and choose a response that maintains the friendship while addressing your concerns. This self-control helps navigate tricky social landscapes, maintaining relationships and personal integrity.

Self-Reflection Prompt: Journaling Your Challenges

The process of writing helps solidify insights, turning them into valuable lessons for future challenges. For this exercise:

1. Reflect on a recent situation where you had to use your executive functions. Write about what happened, how you handled it, and what you learned.
2. Identify times when you successfully prioritized tasks or managed emotions.
3. Consider areas where you struggled and think about what you might do differently next time.

This reflection isn't only about critiquing yourself; it's about recognizing your strengths and understanding areas for growth. As you continue to develop these skills, you'll find that self-reflection becomes a powerful tool, guiding you to make thoughtful decisions and navigate life's complexities with confidence.

IDENTIFYING YOUR STRENGTHS AND WEAKNESSES IN EXECUTIVE SKILLS

Discovering your strengths and weaknesses in executive functioning is like building a personalized toolkit for life. It starts with taking a good look at where you excel and where you might need a little help. To get started, consider using self-assessment questionnaires designed to identify your skills. These tools can give you insight into areas like time management, organization, and focus. But don't stop there. Reflective exercises are another great way to gain self-awareness. Spend some time thinking about past experiences—when did you feel on top of things, and when did you struggle? By taking time to think about these moments, you can pinpoint specific skills to work on.

Once you've identified your strengths and weaknesses, it's time to strategize. You can set achievable goals to strengthen weaker areas.

Break down your objectives into small, manageable steps. Let's say you want to improve your organization. Start by setting a goal to organize your study space. Once you've done that, move on to organizing your digital files. Another effective strategy is to develop organizational systems. Create a filing system for schoolwork or use a calendar app to manage your time better. These systems can become second nature with practice, making life feel more manageable.

Keep in mind that personalized learning is key. Everyone has unique learning styles, so why should you rely on a one-size-fits-all approach? Customize your study methods to suit your style. If you're a visual learner, use diagrams and charts to help you understand complex topics. Prefer to listen to learn? Try recording lectures or discussions and listening to them later. Creating customized schedules that fit your peak productivity times can also make a big difference. Some people work best in the morning, while others find their groove in the afternoon or evening. Experiment to see what works best for you and match your routine to that.

Don't underestimate the power of feedback from others. Peer feedback can be incredibly valuable. Talk with classmates or friends to get different perspectives on your strengths and weaknesses. They might notice something about your work habits that you have yet to see yourself. Peer review sessions are another great tool. When you share your work with others and get constructive feedback, you gain insights that can be transformative. It also builds a sense of community as you learn from and support each other. This collaboration can lead to personal growth and improvement in your executive skills.

Interactive Exercise: Peer Feedback Session

Try organizing a peer feedback session with a group of friends or classmates. Then, follow these steps:

1. Choose a specific skill or project to focus on, whether it's a recent essay, a presentation, or your approach to managing homework.
2. Take turns presenting your work and offer each other constructive feedback.
3. Focus on strengths as well as areas for improvement. Ask questions like, "What did you find most effective?" or "How could I improve this aspect?"
4. By the end of the session, you'll have a clearer picture of your skills and areas to work on. Plus, you'll likely pick up tips from others that you can apply to your own work.

Remember, the goal isn't to criticize but to support each other in becoming the best versions of yourselves.

THE ROLE OF EMOTIONS IN EXECUTIVE FUNCTIONING

Have you ever been asked to present in front of your class unexpectedly? If you're like me, your heart races, your palms sweat, and suddenly, everything you've prepared seems to vanish from your mind. This is where emotions start playing their part in executive functioning. Emotions, whether fear, excitement, or frustration, can influence how well you think and act. Stress, for example, can cloud your decision-making, making it harder to think clearly and choose the best course of action. It might lead you to freeze or make quick decisions without considering all the options.

On the other hand, emotions like motivation can be incredibly beneficial. When you're excited about a project or goal, your brain kicks into high gear, helping you stay focused and persistent. Motivation fuels your ability to complete tasks, even when they're challenging. It's like an engine that keeps you moving forward, ensuring you finish what you start.

Emotion regulation techniques can be a game-changer in managing these mood swings. Mindfulness exercises, which involve focusing on the present moment without judgment, help calm your mind and reduce the anxiety that can mess with your executive functions. Imagine sitting quietly, closing your eyes, and taking deep breaths. You pay attention to your breathing, noticing the sensation of air entering and leaving your body. This simple act of mindfulness can help slow down racing thoughts and bring a sense of calm. Stress management strategies are also important. Think of activities you find relaxing, like drawing, listening to music, or even going for a walk. These can help you manage stress levels, keeping your mind clear and focused.

Emotions are also linked to behavior, which means that how you feel can directly influence how you act. For instance, handling criticism constructively can be challenging, especially if it feels personal. But by managing your emotional response, you can turn criticism into a tool for growth. When someone critiques your work, try pausing to consider their perspective. This thoughtful approach helps you learn from the feedback without taking it as a personal attack.

Similarly, managing frustration in school is essential. It's easy to feel overwhelmed when you need help understanding a topic or struggling with an assignment. But instead of letting frustration take over, try breaking the problem into smaller parts. Tackle each piece one at a time, and celebrate small victories along the way. This method not only helps you complete the task but also builds resilience.

A vital part of improving your executive functioning is being aware of your emotions and their triggers. A *trigger* is something that happens that makes you have a reaction. Start by identifying what stresses you out. Is it a particular subject, social situation, or pressure to perform? Once you know your triggers, you can work on strategies to manage them. Reflecting on your emotional responses also helps. Consider keeping a journal where you jot down how you feel in different situations. Think about what happened, how you reacted, and what you can do differently next time. Understanding these patterns gives you the power to change them. It's like having a roadmap for your emotions, helping you navigate future challenges with greater ease and confidence.

Visual Element: Emotion-Behavior Connection Chart

1. For this exercise, create a simple chart that connects common emotions with potential behaviors.
2. On one side, list emotions like stress, happiness, or frustration.
3. On the opposite side, note behaviors that might result, such as procrastination, focus, or avoidance.

This visual aid can help you see the link between how you feel and how you act, making it easier to address negative patterns and reinforce positive ones.

Recognizing how emotions affect your executive functioning is the first step toward using them to your advantage. With practice, you'll find that managing your feelings doesn't just make you feel better—it can also improve how you think and act in every part of your life.

WHY EXECUTIVE FUNCTIONS MATTER: BEYOND SCHOOL AND INTO LIFE

It's easy to think of executive functions as just another set of skills you need for school, but these abilities reach far beyond the classroom walls. Consider them the keys to navigating life. Take career advancement, for example. As you move from part-time jobs to a long-term career, your ability to plan, manage time, and adapt will be invaluable. Employers value employees who can prioritize tasks, execute projects efficiently, and think critically in high-pressure situations. These skills are your ticket to standing out in competitive environments, where being organized and decisive can lead to promotions and new opportunities.

Executive functions play a vital role in personal relationships, too. Strong interpersonal skills require empathy, patience, and effective communication, all of which are supported by your ability to regulate emotions and think flexibly. Consider the importance of active listening when a friend needs support or the need for compromise when making joint decisions. These interactions require you to manage your responses and adapt to others' needs, ensuring smoother and more meaningful connections. As you strengthen these skills, you'll find it easier to build and maintain relationships, which are crucial for a fulfilling life.

Outside of personal interactions, executive functions can help you handle real-world scenarios like managing finances. Whether budgeting for a summer trip or planning long-term savings, these skills help you set priorities, track expenses, and adjust spending habits. Balancing work-life responsibilities is another area where executive skills shine. As you juggle various commitments—work, family, hobbies—your ability to organize and prioritize becomes your greatest asset. These skills help you use your time wisely, ensuring you meet obligations while still enjoying downtime. It's about creating harmony between different aspects of your life!

The importance of developing executive functions doesn't stop when you're an adult. Lifelong learning is essential in a world that's always changing. Continuing education keeps your skills sharp, whether through formal classes or informal learning experiences. Engaging in lifelong learning opportunities helps you stay relevant in your field and adapt to new challenges. It cultivates curiosity and innovation, ensuring you're always ready for what's next. This ongoing development of executive functions keeps your mind agile and open to new ideas, a vital component for personal and professional growth.

A *growth mindset* is pivotal in this context. It's about seeing challenges as opportunities, not obstacles. Embracing change allows you to adapt and thrive in new situations, whether it's switching jobs, moving to a new city, or starting a new hobby. Building resilience through executive functions helps you recover from setbacks and keep moving forward. This mindset empowers you to take risks, learn from failures, and continuously improve. It's a powerful approach that turns uncertainty into possibility, ensuring you remain adaptable and resourceful, no matter what stage of life you're in.

As you reflect on these ideas, consider how executive functions have already impacted your life. Are there moments when you've successfully navigated a complex situation or managed multiple responsibilities? Recognize the skills you've used and the growth you've experienced. This reflection isn't just about acknowledging past successes but also about identifying areas for future development. Strengthening your executive functions can lead to a more organized, fulfilling, and successful life. Embrace these skills as lifelong allies, guiding you through wherever you are in your personal and professional life.

2

MASTERING TIME MANAGEMENT

Let's start this chapter with a thought experiment: Imagine that time is a giant puzzle. Every piece represents a task, a responsibility, or a moment of relaxation that makes up your day. Without the bigger picture, this puzzle can feel overwhelming and chaotic. But with the right strategy (like the image on the box), you can fit the pieces together smoothly. Welcome to the chapter where we tackle this puzzle of time management head-on. It's not about filling every minute with productive tasks; it's about creating a balanced schedule that works how you need it to. We'll explore how to craft a personalized daily schedule that empowers you to make the most of your time; it will help you reduce stress and boost productivity. Whether you're balancing school, hobbies, or downtime, a well-structured schedule can make a big difference in how you approach each day.

Creating your personalized daily schedule begins with understanding your peak productivity hours. Everyone has times when they feel most alert and focused. Maybe the morning is when your brain is sharpest; others might find that they can get more done in the afternoon or evening. Identifying your best time can help you schedule tasks that require more concentration. But it's not just about work!

It's also crucial to make time for breaks and relaxation. Think of breaks as mini-recharges for your brain. They help you stay energized throughout the day and prevent burnout. Whether it's a quick walk outside, listening to your favorite music, or simply closing your eyes for a few minutes, these moments of rest help keep you at your best.

Prioritization is another aspect of effective scheduling. You can't do everything all at once, so you need to decide what needs your attention first. This is where you can use a tool called the Eisenhower Box. Named after Dwight D. Eisenhower, this method helps you prioritize tasks by dividing them into four categories:

- urgent and important
- important but not urgent
- urgent but not important
- neither urgent nor important

By putting each task in one of the categories, you can focus on what matters the most and avoid getting distracted by less critical tasks. This method not only boosts your efficiency but also ensures that you're spending time on what aligns with your goals and values.

As a teen, you know that life isn't always predictable. While a structured schedule is helpful, you also need to be flexible. Unexpected events and opportunities have a way of cropping up, and being too rigid can lead to unnecessary stress. That's why it's important to incorporate buffer times into your schedule for tasks that pop up. This lets you adapt without throwing off your entire day. This also lets you stay open to adjusting your plans for spontaneous opportunities, like a last-minute invite to hang out with friends or a sudden need to help at home. Remember, a flexible schedule doesn't mean you're disciplined; it means you have the foresight to plan for the unexpected.

Building a routine is another powerful strategy in time management. Establishing consistent daily habits enhances your productivity by creating a rhythm your body and mind can follow. Morning rituals set the tone for your day. Whether it's a quick workout, reading, or simply enjoying a quiet breakfast, these activities can boost your mood and energy levels. In the same way, evening wind-down activities help signal to your brain that it's time to relax and get ready for sleep. This could be as simple as reading a book, journaling about your day, or practicing meditation. Routine doesn't mean boring; it's about setting a foundation that supports your well-being and success.

INTERACTIVE ELEMENT: TASK PRIORITIZATION EXERCISE

Try this exercise to practice using the Eisenhower Box:

1. Write down all the tasks you need to accomplish this week.
2. Then, draw a box with four quadrants. Label them as follows:
    - "Urgent and Important"
    - "Important but Not Urgent"
    - "Urgent but Not Important"
    - "Neither Urgent nor Important"
3. Place each task in the appropriate category.
4. Focus first on completing tasks in the "Urgent and Important" quadrant and plan time for those in "Important but Not Urgent."
5. Reflect on how this helps make your priorities more clear and use your time more effectively.

Mastering time management is about finding what works best for you, and it might take a bit of trial and error. The goal is to create a schedule that makes you the most productive *and* leaves room for joy and relaxation.

USING TECHNOLOGY TO TAME PROCRASTINATION

If you're like most of us, your phone is practically an extension of your hand, so let's use it to our advantage! Using technology is a game-changer for managing time and avoiding procrastination. Imagine having a personal assistant in your pocket, always ready to remind you of deadlines and help organize your tasks. That's precisely what productivity apps like Todoist and Google Calendar can do for you. Todoist offers a simple interface where you can list tasks, set priorities, and even break big projects into smaller, manageable steps. On the other hand, Google Calendar is perfect for scheduling your day, setting reminders, and visualizing your week at a glance. With these tools, you're not just keeping track of what needs to be done; you're actively planning how to tackle each task.

As helpful as these digital tools are, it's easy to get sidetracked by the very technology that's supposed to help you. Notifications pinging every few minutes can pull you away from your focus. This is where you need to set digital boundaries. Start by turning off all the notifications that aren't totally necessary. Do you really need to know the second someone likes your photo or when a new episode of your favorite podcast drops? Probably not. Set app usage limits on your smartphone to keep tabs on how much time you're spending on non-productive activities. Use your phone's settings to schedule downtime, where only essential apps are accessible. It's all about creating a digital space that supports your goals rather than distracts from them.

To make it even easier to focus, consider tech-assisted techniques that help you concentrate. Apps like Forest are designed to keep you on track by turning focus into a game. You plant a virtual tree, and it grows while you stay off your phone. The longer you focus, the more your forest thrives. It's a fun way to visualize your progress while keeping your attention on the task at hand. Browser extensions can also be incredibly helpful for blocking distracting sites. If you find yourself constantly wandering to social media or other time-wasting websites, extensions like StayFocusd can limit the amount of time you spend there, gently nudging you back to your work.

But while technology can be a fantastic aid, it's important not to let screens take over your life entirely. Regular tech breaks are good for your mental clarity. Your brain needs a breather from the constant stream of digital information. Try to assign screen-free zones in your daily routine. This could be as simple as deciding not to use your phone while you eat or dedicating the first hour after you wake up to offline activities. Scheduling tech-free time allows you to recharge and refresh your mind. Plus, it helps you be more productive when you return to your tasks. Think about activities that don't involve screens, like reading a book, going for a walk, and practicing a hobby. These breaks not only rest your eyes but also stimulate creativity and reduce stress, keeping your mental health in check.

These strategies can transform how you interact with technology. It's not just about cutting out distractions; it's about using technology as a tool to enhance your productivity and focus. By being mindful about how much time you spend online and setting boundaries, you're creating a more balanced digital life. Plus, regular breaks ensure you're working smarter, not harder, keeping both your mind and body in peak condition.

THE POMODORO TECHNIQUE: BOOSTING PRODUCTIVITY

Picture this: You're staring at your math homework, but your mind keeps wandering to that new video game or your friends' latest group chat. It's tough to stay focused, right? Let me tell you about the Pomodoro Technique, a simple yet powerful method to help you zero in on your work and get stuff done. Named after the Italian word for "tomato" (because of the tomato-shaped timer its creator used), this technique breaks work into manageable chunks, transforming your study sessions into focused sprints. Here's how it works:

1. You set a timer for 25 minutes and dive deep into your task, giving it your full attention.
2. When the timer rings, you take a 5-minute break—grab a snack, stretch, or just breathe.

Simple, right? This cycle is designed to keep your mind sharp and your motivation high because these short bursts of work prevent fatigue and fight procrastination.

It's not difficult to use the Pomodoro Technique, but it does require a bit of planning. Here's how to do it:

1. Start by listing tasks you want to tackle with your Pomodoro sessions. Choose clear and specific tasks, like "read two chapters" or "solve ten math problems."
2. Once your list is ready, set your timer for 25 minutes and begin.
3. Focus solely on the task at hand, resisting the urge to multitask or check your phone.
4. When the timer goes off, mark a check next to your task to track your progress.
5. After four Pomodoros, take a longer break—15 to 30 minutes. Use this time to recharge before diving back into your work.

This structured approach helps you make the most of your study time and gives you a sense of accomplishment as you check items off your list.

The Pomodoro Technique has its perks, but like any method, it comes with its challenges. One of the biggest benefits is improved focus. By working in short, intense bursts, you train your brain to concentrate more deeply and avoid distractions. Plus, the regular breaks help prevent burnout, keeping your energy levels steady throughout the day. However, some people find it hard to get back into it after a break, especially if they're in the zone when the timer rings. It can feel disruptive to stop, but remember that these breaks are essential for maintaining overall productivity. If it feels like you're taking breaks too often, tweak the technique to better suit your unique rhythm.

Customize the Pomodoro Technique to make it work for you. While the traditional method uses 25-minute sessions, you might find that different intervals work better. Maybe you prefer working for 45 minutes with a 10-minute break, or shorter sessions keep you more engaged. Experiment with different timing to find what is best for your concentration levels. You could also try taking longer breaks after completing multiple Pomodoros to give yourself a longer rest period. This can be especially helpful during intense study periods or when preparing for exams, allowing you to recharge more thoroughly before tackling the next round of work.

Visual Element: Pomodoro Tracker Template

Create or print a simple Pomodoro tracker template. Include columns for task names, Pomodoro sessions, and break times. Use it to plan your study sessions and track how many Pomodoros you complete each day. This visual representation of your progress can be incredibly motivating, as it highlights how much you're accomplishing with each focused session. Plus, it helps you identify patterns in your productivity, allowing you to adjust your strategy as needed.

BALANCING ACADEMICS AND EXTRACURRICULARS WITH EASE

Balancing academics with extracurricular activities can sometimes feel like juggling bowling balls while riding a unicycle. But it doesn't have to be that way! The key is to create a system that lets you shine in your studies and pursue your passions. Start with a weekly planner. This tool will help you visualize your commitments and find time for everything you love. Assign specific time slots for each activity, whether it's practice for the soccer team, band rehearsals, or that language club you joined. By dedicating time to each, you ensure nothing falls through the cracks and you're not scrambling at the last minute. This will help you stress less and enjoy each activity fully.

It's also important to find the right balance between schoolwork and extracurriculars. This keeps you from burning out and ensures you're growing in all areas of your life. When you spread yourself too thin, it's easy to feel overwhelmed, which can make you feel exhausted or even lose interest in activities you once enjoyed. Balance helps prevent this by making time for personal growth and development. This broad approach allows you to develop skills like leadership, teamwork, and communication—which will benefit you in school and beyond. Not to mention, by participating in activities you're passionate about, you gain experiences that make you a more well-rounded person.

One effective strategy to maintain this balance is time blocking. Have you heard of it? It involves setting aside specific blocks of time for different activities. You might reserve the afternoons for homework and studies, leaving evenings free for sports or arts. Maybe you dedicate Saturday mornings to volunteer work, while Sundays are for rest and family. Time blocking helps you focus on one task at a time, reducing the urge to multitask and increasing your productivity. By clearly defining these blocks, you get rid of the stress of deciding what to do next, freeing up mental space for more creative and productive thoughts. This method can transform your chaotic schedule into a well-oiled machine.

Regularly reviewing your commitments is another essential aspect of maintaining balance. Life is dynamic, and so are your priorities. Set aside time each week to reflect on your schedule. Are you feeling overwhelmed or stretched too thin? It might be time to adjust your commitments. You may need to drop an activity that no longer excites you or shift your focus to something new. Weekly reflection sessions are an opportunity to reassess your goals and ensure your schedule includes what truly matters to you. As you review, consider upcoming events that might require extra time or energy and adjust your priorities accordingly.

Keeping a balance between academics and extracurriculars isn't only about managing time; it's about making sure that each aspect of your life complements the others. By creating a system that supports your interests and responsibilities, you can excel in school, enjoy your hobbies, and still have time to relax. The skills you develop through this process—time management, prioritization, and self-awareness—will serve you well throughout your life. So, embrace the challenge of balancing it all!

WEEKEND PLANNING: MAXIMIZING YOUR FREE TIME

Weekends can feel like a breath of fresh air after a busy week—they're your chance to recharge and prepare for what's next. But without a plan, they can slip by without you even noticing. That's why it's important to plan your weekend, too! Start by listing out your weekend goals. What do you want to accomplish? Maybe it's finishing a book, catching up on some schoolwork, or simply relaxing. Once you have a list, you can organize your time to fit everything in. Make sure to schedule activities you enjoy. Whether it's a movie night with friends or a nature hike, these moments of joy are just as important as ticking off tasks. A good balance ensures you're refreshed and ready for Monday.

Balancing work and play isn't just about dividing your time; it's about getting the best of both worlds. Planning fun outings with friends is a great way to unwind and build stronger connections. But don't forget about your chores! Setting aside time for these tasks means you won't spend Sunday night in a mad dash to get everything done. It's about creating harmony between relaxation and responsibility so you can enjoy your weekend without the looming dread of unfinished work. This balance gives you the chance to breathe, laugh, and still feel productive.

Weekends are also a perfect time for personal growth. Why not use some of your free hours to learn something new? Picking up a hobby, like playing an instrument or learning to cook, can be incredibly rewarding. Have you ever considered volunteering in your community? Not only does this help others, but it also builds skills and experiences that can enrich your life. These activities contribute to your development in ways that textbooks can't, providing a different kind of learning that's both fun and fulfilling. Personal growth doesn't have to be a chore; it can be an exciting part of your weekend.

Reflection and planning can turn a good weekend into a great one. Use this time to think about the past week. What went well? What could have been better? Journaling these reflections can give you valuable insights into your habits and how you can improve. It's a chance to learn from your experiences and make changes for the future. After reflecting, create a rough plan for the week ahead. This doesn't have to be detailed, but having a general idea of your priorities can help you start the week with a clear mind. By planning ahead, you reduce stress and set yourself up for success.

OVERCOMING LAST-MINUTE CRAMMING: PLANNING FOR EXAMS

Test time often feels like a looming storm cloud. When it hits, the temptation to cram can be overwhelming. But here's the thing: Cramming rarely leads to success, no matter what we try to tell ourselves. Instead of solidifying information, it often results in increased stress levels and poor retention. When you cram, you're trying to stuff your brain with too much information at once, which can lead to mental fatigue and confusion. You might remember details for a short while, but long-term memory suffers. It's like trying to fill a suitcase by just throwing everything in—sure, you might get it closed, but you won't find what you need when you arrive.

Instead of cramming, take some time to come up with an effective study plan. The key is breaking down subjects into manageable sections. Think of it like splitting your study material into bite-sized pieces. Start by identifying the main topics for each subject, then divide them into smaller chunks you can tackle over several weeks. Creating a study timeline is another vital step. Map out when you'll focus on each section leading up to the exam. This way, you give yourself plenty of time to review and avoid the last-minute rush. Consistency is crucial here. Following a timeline allows you to pace yourself, ensuring you cover all necessary material without feeling overwhelmed.

Active learning techniques can also transform your study sessions. Passive reading might seem easy, but it doesn't engage your brain as effectively. Instead, try using flashcards when you study. They're a fantastic tool for testing your knowledge and reinforcing key concepts. Write down important terms or questions on one side, with answers on the other. This method helps your active recall, which strengthens your memory. Joining study groups is another excellent strategy. Discussing topics with peers allows you to hear different perspectives, which can deepen your understanding. Plus, teaching someone else is one of the best ways to reinforce your own learning.

Regular review sessions are another great test-prep strategy. Don't wait until the night before the test to start reviewing. Instead, schedule weekly reviews of key concepts. This helps move the information from your short-term to your long-term memory. Incorporate past exam papers into these sessions. Practicing with real questions gets you familiar with the format and shows you areas where you need more focus. It's like having a dress rehearsal before the big performance, ensuring you're comfortable and confident when it counts. This approach to studying doesn't only prepare you for exams —it builds a foundation for lifelong learning.

By making these changes, you replace the stress of cramming with a well-organized plan that boosts your confidence and performance. You'll find that when test day arrives, you're not just ready; you're confidently prepared to show what you know. These strategies improve your grades and develop skills that you can take to college and beyond. Each exam becomes an opportunity to demonstrate your hard-earned knowledge and skills rather than a source of anxiety.

As we wrap up this chapter on mastering time management, remember that these skills are your allies in navigating the demands of school and life. From creating practical study plans to balancing your commitments, you gain control over your time and energy. This foundation sets the stage for exploring the next chapter, where we'll dive into organizational skills that further support your academic and personal success.

3

ORGANIZATIONAL SKILLS FOR SUCCESS

Imagine that your brain is a cluttered desk piled high with papers, notebooks, and sticky notes. You know there's important stuff in there, but finding it can feel like searching for a single sheet in a mountain of chaos. This chapter is all about transforming that clutter into order. By mastering organizational skills, you can create systems that help you find what you need when you need it without the stress of losing track. We'll explore the world of digital tools, which are like having a virtual assistant at your fingertips. These tools can simplify your life and make it easier to keep everything in its place, from school notes to important documents.

DIGITAL ORGANIZATION: MANAGING FILES AND NOTES

We live in a tech-savvy world, so digital tools are your best allies in staying organized. Platforms like Google Drive are fantastic for storing all your files in one place. With cloud storage, you can access your documents from any device, whether you're at home, school, or anywhere else life takes you. This means no more panicking when you realize you left your homework on your laptop at home. Everything is securely stored online, ready whenever you need it.

Plus, using a platform like Google Drive gets rid of physical clutter and frees up space in your backpack or desk.

Note-taking apps like Evernote can change the way you capture and organize information. Evernote lets you create digital notebooks that you can sort into folders, which makes it easy to divide up notes by subject or project. You can also use apps like Notability or Google Keep, which are tailored for students and offer features like audio recordings and photo integration. You can use these tools to enhance your notes with multimedia. It's so much easier to record a teacher's explanation or snap a picture of a complicated diagram! This helps you remember the information and makes studying more interactive and engaging.

Creating a digital filing system might seem daunting, but it's simpler than you think. Start by setting up folders for each subject or project, and use subfolders for specific topics or types of documents. This makes it easy to locate what you need without sifting through a digital pile. Make sure you use a consistent system when naming your files. For instance, label files with the date and a brief description, like "2023-10-12_History_Project" or "Math_Notes_Chapter5." This will make it so you can quickly identify what each file is without having to open it.

With all this technology at your fingertips, it's also essential to take notes effectively. Start by using bullet points to organize information logically. Highlight key concepts or terms, either with bold text or colored markers available in your app. Adding images and audio can also bring your notes to life. If you're studying biology, a photo of a cell structure or a recording of your teacher explaining a complex concept can make a big difference. These techniques turn your notes from words on a screen into a comprehensive resource for studying.

Finally, remember to protect your digital files. Regularly back up your documents to prevent data loss in case something goes wrong. You can set up automatic backups through services like Google Drive, which can sync your files across devices. This way, even if you accidentally delete something, you can recover it easily. Security is equally important. Use strong, unique passwords for your cloud accounts and enable two-factor authentication for an extra layer of protection. Encryption tools can also protect sensitive information. These steps ensure your digital life remains secure, giving you peace of mind and protecting your hard work.

Interactive Element: Digital Organization Challenge

Create a digital organization challenge for yourself. This challenge helps you get organized and builds skills that will serve you throughout your academic and personal life. Here's what to do:

1. Spend a week setting up your digital filing system, using folders and naming conventions to sort your files.
2. Experiment with a new note-taking app, trying out bullet points and multimedia features.
3. At the end of the week, evaluate how these changes have impacted your organization and efficiency.
4. Reflect on what worked well and what could be improved.

DECLUTTERING YOUR SPACE: A STEP-BY-STEP GUIDE

Let's move from the digital realm to somewhere closer to home: your bedroom. How do you feel when you go to your room? Imagine walking in and feeling instantly relaxed, not overwhelmed by the chaos of clothes, books, and random bits of paper scattered everywhere. A clutter-free environment doesn't only look nice—it helps clear your mind and makes it easier to focus and be creative. When your space is organized, distractions fade away, and you can concentrate on what truly matters, like studying for that big test or working on your latest art project. You might be surprised at how much more you can accomplish when you're not constantly searching for lost items or tripping over clutter. Plus, having a tidy space can boost your mood, making it a place you actually want to spend time in.

Getting to that state of zen might seem daunting, but with a solid plan, it's totally doable. Let's look at one way to get it done:

1. Start by sorting your belongings into three piles:
    - keep
    - donate
    - discard
2. This method helps you make decisions about what's necessary and what's just taking up space.
3. Set a timer for each session to keep yourself focused and prevent burnout. Maybe start with 30-minute increments, tackling one area at a time, like your desk or closet.
4. If you find something you haven't used in months, it's probably safe to say it can go.

Letting go of unnecessary items can feel liberating and make room for the things you truly value. Remember, the goal is to keep only what serves a purpose or brings you joy.

Once you've cleared out the clutter, think about how to organize what's left. Storage bins and shelving units can be lifesavers, and you can use them to designate a spot for everything. Labeling containers is a simple yet effective way to know exactly where everything belongs, which will save you time when you need to find something quickly. You could have bins labeled "School Supplies," "Craft Materials," or "Sports Gear." This system keeps your space looking neat and makes it easy for you to stay organized. Shelves can display your favorite books or collectibles, adding a personal touch while keeping things tidy. With a bit of creativity, you can transform your space into a functional and aesthetically pleasing haven.

One thing to remember is that creating a clutter-free environment isn't just a one-time task; it's a habit to maintain over time. Schedule regular decluttering days, maybe once a month, to reassess and reorganize as needed. This keeps things from piling up again. Another helpful rule is the "one in, one out" approach. It works like this: if you bring in something new, like a pair of shoes or a gadget, get rid of something old. This helps manage your possessions and keeps things from piling up. These habits ensure that your space remains a sanctuary of calm and productivity. It becomes a place where you can think clearly and feel inspired. Regular maintenance might seem like a chore, but it pays off by creating an environment that supports your goals and well-being.

Textual Element: Reflection Section

Take a moment and think of a space in your room that feels cluttered. How does it make you feel? How would decluttering this area improve your daily life? Write down three specific steps you can take to organize this space. For example, you might sort through your desk drawers, organize your bookshelf, or clear off your nightstand. Choose one or two items you're ready to let go of. Think about how these changes might impact your focus and creativity. Answering these questions can motivate you to make the changes needed for a more organized and peaceful environment.

COLOR CODING AND LABELING: TOOLS FOR EFFICIENCY

Color coding and labeling might sound like something from a craft project, but they're powerful tools for organizing your life. Imagine having a toolbox where each tool is color-coded. It would make it easy to find precisely what you need without rummaging through the whole box, right? That's the beauty of color coding. Assigning colors to different subjects or categories can transform your chaotic notes into a visually appealing system that's easy to make sense of. You could use a specific color for each subject in school—red for math, blue for science, green for history—and apply it consistently across your folders, binders, and even digital files. This makes finding what you need quicker and helps your brain associate colors with specific topics, making you more efficient.

Labeling takes this organization a step further. A clear, informative label is like a signpost, guiding you directly to what you need. When creating labels, the key is to be consistent. Use the same format across all your materials, whether it's the font size or the information included. For example, a label on your binder might have the subject name, your class period, and the teacher's name. This way, even if you're in a rush, you'll know exactly which binder to grab. And labels aren't just for school materials; they can also be used in your personal spaces. Imagine opening your closet and seeing everything neatly labeled—shelves for "Winter Wear," "Sports Gear," or "Casual Outfits." It might sound extreme, but these small steps can save you a ton of time and stress, especially when you're in a hurry.

Color coding and labeling can be game-changers at school, too. Think about your school binder. Instead of flipping through pages to find the right section, color-coded dividers can guide you instantly. You could have a purple section for language arts, yellow for math, and so on. Labeled dividers in your notebooks can separate class notes, homework, and test reviews, making it easier to study and stay prepared. When you use these techniques consistently, you create a system that works seamlessly, reducing the time you spend searching for information and increasing the time you have to actually get work done.

While it is important to be practical, there's no reason your organizational system can't reflect your personal style. Personalization makes organizing feel less like a chore and more like an expression of who you are. Maybe you're into neon colors or prefer pastels—use your favorite colors in your system. Design custom labels with unique fonts or patterns that make you smile. Incorporate themes that speak to you, whether it's your favorite movie, hobby, or even colors that match your room. When you love how your organizational tools look, you're more likely to use them consistently, which is the ultimate goal. Plus, sharing your creative systems with friends can inspire them to get organized, too, turning a seemingly boring task into a fun experience together.

BACKPACK AND LOCKER MANAGEMENT 101

Your backpack is more than just a bag; it's your mobile command center. The way you organize it can make or break your school day. Start by thinking of your backpack like a house with different rooms for various activities. Use compartments to organize items by category. Keep all writing utensils in one pocket, snacks in another, and notebooks in the main compartment. This approach ensures you can avoid digging through a jumble of stuff to find what you need. Keep heavier items close to your back so you can balance and be more comfortable. Regularly clean out unnecessary items. Those crumpled papers and old wrappers? Toss them. This frees up space and lightens your load, making it easier to find essential items quickly. A well-organized backpack can reduce the daily stress of searching for things, giving you more time to focus on what matters.

Much like your backpack, your locker is like a home base at school, and keeping it organized can save you from frantic searches between classes. Think about installing shelves or using organizers to make use of the space. You could use a locker shelf for books and another for supplies, arranging them by how often you use them. Keep your most-used items within easy reach so you're not wasting precious minutes digging through your locker. Consider arranging books vertically, like a mini-library, which makes it easier to spot the titles and grab what you need. Hooks inside the door can hold your jacket or gym bag, keeping the floor clear. An organized locker means you can grab what you need and go, letting you manage those hectic transitions between classes with ease.

Staying organized requires daily habits that might seem small but make a big difference. Each evening, take a few minutes to check your backpack. Find what you need for the next day's classes, and remove anything you don't. This habit not only prepares you for the day ahead but also reduces morning chaos. You can also schedule weekly locker cleanouts. Set aside time, maybe every Friday, to tidy up and reassess your locker's contents. This consistent upkeep prevents clutter from building up and ensures your locker remains a functional space.

When your backpack and locker are organized, it's not just about neatness. It significantly impacts your stress levels and focus. Knowing that everything has its place means you have quick access to materials during class, so you're staying focused on not having to search for a missing pen or textbook. An organized space means your mind can focus on learning rather than where you put that assignment or whether you forgot a book at home. This clarity translates into better concentration and a more relaxed attitude toward your school day.

CREATING A HOMEWORK COMMAND CENTER

What if you could have a specific spot where your brain switches into homework mode every time you sit down? That's the beauty of a homework command center. It's your personal headquarters for tackling school tasks, a space dedicated solely to learning and productivity. This isn't just a desk with a pile of books; it's a well-organized, comfortable spot where you can focus and get things done. What's the key to a successful command center? Having essential supplies and tools within reach. Think about what you often need: pencils, pens, highlighters, sticky notes, and maybe even a calculator. Having these tools near you means no more getting up every few minutes to grab something, which can break your concentration.

Setting up your homework command center is all about finding the right spot. Choose a quiet corner of your room where there are few distractions. Natural light is a bonus because it can enhance focus and reduce eye strain. Once you've picked a spot, organize your supplies. Use desk organizers or small baskets to sort items. Keep your most-used supplies in an easy-to-reach spot and keep everything else in drawers or on shelves. The goal is to create a clutter-free environment where everything has a designated place, making it easy to stay organized and quickly find what you need.

Here are the advantages of having a dedicated homework space: First, it improves concentration. Knowing that this spot is meant for work helps train your mind to focus when you're there. It's like having a mental switch that shifts you into study mode. A homework command center also creates a clear separation between study and play areas. This separation is important for a healthy school-life balance. When you finish your tasks, you can leave the space and truly relax, knowing your work is done.

Personalize your homework space to make it a place you enjoy spending time in. Add motivational posters or quotes that inspire you to push through challenging assignments. These reminders give you a quick boost when you're feeling stuck. If possible, find some comfortable furniture to help you get through long study sessions. An adjustable chair and a desk at the right height can make a big difference in your posture and comfort level. Personal touches, like a small plant or a family photo, can make the space feel inviting and uniquely yours. The more comfortable and personalized your command center is, the more motivated you'll be to use it.

SYNCING CALENDARS AND TO-DO LISTS FOR ULTIMATE CONTROL

Even with all of this organization, keeping track of your tasks and schedules can feel like juggling flaming swords. But with the right tools, you can manage everything smoothly. We talked about how digital calendars like Outlook or Apple Calendar are lifesavers, helping you easily organize your day-to-day activities. You can color-code events, set reminders, and even send invites for group projects. Meanwhile, to-do list apps like Microsoft To Do offer a structured way to keep track of your tasks. With features like "My Day," you can focus on specific tasks without feeling overwhelmed. These apps are designed to simplify your life and give you a clear view of what's essential and when it needs to be done.

A key step to remember is to sync your calendars and to-do lists across your devices. Whether you're on your phone, tablet, or computer, having your schedule and tasks at your fingertips ensures you never miss a beat. Start by setting up cloud synchronization, which lets you update once and see those changes everywhere. This way, if you add a new assignment on your phone, it automatically updates on your laptop. Enable notifications and reminders to help you stay on top of deadlines and remind you of upcoming tasks or events. This way, you don't have to juggle multiple schedules.

Integrating your calendar and to-do list tools makes it easier to manage your time. Creating task-specific calendar events allows you to visualize your workload and allocate time efficiently. For example, if you have a group project due, you can schedule blocks of time dedicated to research, writing, and revising. Linking tasks to deadlines and appointments gives you a clear picture of what needs to be done and when. This planning helps you avoid last-minute scrambles and reduces anxiety, allowing you to manage your time with confidence.

The magic of effective scheduling doesn't stop at organizing your tasks. Regular reviews and updates help maintain an accurate and efficient schedule. Weekly planning sessions give you the chance to look at your progress and make adjustments. During these sessions, you can think about what you've accomplished and identify areas that need more focus. Daily task reviews help you stay on track, allowing you to adjust priorities based on changes in your schedule. This ongoing evaluation ensures you remain proactive, adapting to new challenges as they arise.

Ultimately, combining synced calendars and to-do lists is the ultimate cheat code for managing your life. These tools organize your tasks and empower you to take control of your time. Using technology in your routine allows you to streamline daily activities, leaving you with more energy to devote to what truly matters. With a clear understanding of your commitments, you're free to focus on achieving your goals without the constant worry of forgetting something important.

As we close this chapter on organizational skills, think about how these tools and strategies can transform your daily routine. From digital organization to creating a homework command center, these techniques equip you to handle tasks easily and efficiently. With your organizational skills sharpened you're ready to tackle challenges confidently, setting the stage for the next chapter on beating procrastination.

4

BEATING PROCRASTINATION

Picture this: It's the night before a big project is due, and instead of working, you find yourself stuck in the endless scroll of social media or binge-watching your favorite TV show. Sound familiar? This is the frustrating dance of procrastination, a struggle many of us know all too well. It's not just about putting things off; it's about understanding why we do it and how we can stop. Procrastination isn't laziness. It's a complex behavior that's linked to our emotions and thoughts. By exploring what causes procrastination, you can start to see your patterns and make changes.

One of the biggest culprits behind procrastination is the fear of failure. This fear can paralyze you, making the idea of starting a task overwhelming because you might not meet expectations. When you feel like you have to be perfect, it's easier to avoid the task altogether. This is called *perfectionism*. Perfectionism sets impossibly high standards, and when you fear you won't meet them, procrastination becomes a way to escape that pressure. You might tell yourself, "I'll start when I can do it perfectly," which often means never starting at all. This perfectionist mindset can affect your schoolwork and your mental health, creating a cycle of stress and avoidance.

The emotional causes of procrastination run deep. Anxiety often leads to procrastination. The thought of doing a task causes discomfort, leading you to avoid it. You might distract yourself with small tasks to escape this discomfort, but this only delays the inevitable. Avoidance becomes a habit, making it harder to face the task later. Low self-esteem can also play a role. If you doubt your abilities, you might procrastinate to avoid dealing with those doubts. This lack of confidence can make even simple tasks seem impossible, leading you to put them off until the last moment. It's a vicious cycle that can spiral out of control if you don't address it.

Just like every person is different, there are different types of procrastination. *Avoidant procrastination* is when you shy away from tasks because of discomfort or fear of failure. You might find yourself cleaning your room or organizing your desk instead of tackling your homework, using these activities as a distraction. On the other hand, *arousal procrastination* involves waiting until the last minute to start tasks because you believe you work better under pressure. This can lead to a rush of adrenaline that makes you feel productive, but it often leads to stress and poor work. To combat procrastination, you need to first understand your procrastination style.

Self-reflection is a powerful tool in overcoming procrastination. Start by keeping a journal where you keep track of your procrastination. Note what tasks you avoided, how you felt, and what you did instead. This can help you identify patterns and triggers in your behavior. Reflective questions can help you understand even better. Ask yourself why you avoided a task or how you felt about it. Did you fear failure? Were you feeling overwhelmed? By digging into these questions, you can uncover the emotional roots of your procrastination and begin to address them.

INTERACTIVE ELEMENT: JOURNALING PROMPT

Grab a journal and spend a few minutes each day reflecting on your procrastination habits. Here's what to do:

1. Write about a task you delayed.
2. What emotions did you experience?
3. How did you distract yourself?
4. Consider what you could do differently next time.

This exercise isn't about judgment; it's about understanding your behavior and finding ways to change it. The more you practice self-reflection, the more patterns you'll notice, giving you the insight you need to take control and make positive changes in your daily life.

SETTING SMALL WINS: BUILDING MOMENTUM WITH MINI-GOALS

Imagine you're staring at a mountain of homework, but you feel stuck and unsure of where to start. Instead of tackling it all at once, break it down into smaller, more manageable tasks, much like the SMART goals we've discussed. This is where setting mini-goals comes in. You can make progress without feeling overwhelmed by dividing big tasks into sub-tasks. For example, if you have a research paper due, start with finding sources, then create an outline, and then write a draft. Each step is a mini-goal that builds momentum as you check it off your list. These small wins give you a sense of accomplishment and motivate you to keep going.

Creating a goal hierarchy is like building a roadmap for your tasks. This helps you prioritize what's most important and aligns your mini-goals with your larger goals. Here's how to do it:

1. Begin by listing your tasks and organizing them by importance. What needs your immediate attention? What can wait?
2. This prioritization ensures you're focusing on the tasks that matter most.
3. Align these mini-goals with your more significant aims, like improving grades or completing a project on time.

By connecting small tasks to larger goals, you maintain a clear vision of what you're working toward. This approach keeps you on track and helps you see the bigger picture.

Now, let's talk about rewards. Who doesn't love a good reward after getting something done? Using a reward system is a great way to stay motivated. Think about what you enjoy—a favorite snack, a short break to watch a funny video or a quick game on your phone. These personalized rewards can make the work feel less daunting. Timing is important, though. Reward yourself immediately after completing a mini-goal to make the most impact. This instant gratification strengthens the association between effort and reward, encouraging you to enthusiastically tackle the following task.

Tracking your progress lets you know how far you've come and what still needs attention. You can use progress charts to visualize your achievements. Whether it's a simple checklist or a colorful chart, seeing your progress can be incredibly motivating. Look back on your weekly accomplishments to find what worked and what didn't. This helps you adjust your strategies and improve your approach. Regular progress tracking isn't just about staying organized; it's about celebrating your achievements, no matter how small. It reinforces the idea that you're capable of achieving your goals, which will boost your confidence and keep procrastination at bay.

Interactive Element: Mini-Goal Planner

Create a mini-goal planner to organize your tasks. This planner helps you stay organized and keeps you motivated to tackle even the most daunting tasks:

1. Start by listing a big task, like a project or assignment.
2. Break it down into smaller steps, and assign a reward for each completed step.
3. Use a simple chart to track your progress and celebrate your achievements.

4. Reflect on the process at the end of each week to see what you've accomplished and how you can improve.

PROCRASTINATION BUSTERS: TECHNIQUES THAT WORK

Procrastination often feels like an invisible force holding you back, but there are ways to break free from its grip. Let's explore some techniques that can help you get started on tasks and maintain momentum:

The "Two-Minute Rule" is a simple strategy that works wonders. The idea is that if something will take two minutes or less, do it right now. This helps you knock out small tasks before they pile up and become overwhelming. It's surprising how much you can accomplish with this rule—respond to an email, organize your desk, or even jot down a quick note.

Another powerful tool is the "Five-Second Rule." For this rule, you have to act on an impulse within five seconds before your brain convinces you to put it off. When you have the urge to start a task, count down from five and start doing it before doubt sets in. This technique helps you get around the mental noise that often fuels procrastination. It's about creating a sense of urgency to take immediate action. It's especially handy for tasks you know you should do but keep putting off because they seem too difficult.

Changing your thought patterns is another way to tackle procrastination. *Cognitive restructuring* means you reframe negative thoughts that might be holding you back. Instead of thinking, "I'll never finish this project," try shifting to, "I can tackle this one step at a time." This positive mindset can change how you approach tasks and make them feel more manageable.

Visualizing positive outcomes is also beneficial. Picture yourself completing the task and enjoying the benefits of finishing it. This mental image can motivate you to start and keep going because it shifts your focus from obstacles to possibilities.

Environmental adjustments can play a big role in beating procrastination. We touched on this when we talked about creating your command center. Create distraction-free zones that will help you focus. Get rid of items that tend to grab your attention, like your phone or unrelated books. Organize your workspace so everything you need is within reach. A tidy, efficient setup reduces the time spent searching for materials and keeps your focus on your work. This environment creates calm and control, making it easier to concentrate. Simple changes, like good lighting or a comfortable chair, can also go a long way.

Setting *time-bound challenges* is a fun and effective way to boost your productivity. Use timers to set specific periods for work sessions. Implement the Pomodoro Technique we talked about to help maintain concentration and prevent burnout. Competing against yourself can also be motivating. Challenge yourself to beat the clock by completing a task in a certain amount of time. This creates a sense of urgency that can push you to work more efficiently. It's like turning productivity into a game where you're both the competitor and the champion.

Textual Element: Procrastination Challenge Checklist

Create a checklist to tackle procrastination with these techniques:

1. Include actions like:
    - "Apply the Two-Minute Rule"
    - "Use the Five-Second Rule"
    - "Reframe Negative Thoughts"
    - "Visualize Success"
    - "Create a Distraction-Free Zone"
    - "Organize Workspace"
    - "Set a Timer for 25 Minutes"
    - "Challenge Yourself to Beat the Clock"

2. Use this checklist to experiment with different strategies and see what works best for you.

As you try each technique, note how it affects your productivity and which ones you find most helpful. This process of trial and error will help you build a personalized toolkit for overcoming procrastination. Each checkmark represents a step closer to mastering the art of getting things done, transforming procrastination from a barrier into a stepping stone.

ACCOUNTABILITY PARTNERS: HOW FRIENDS CAN HELP YOU STAY ON TRACK

Imagine having a buddy who not only cheers you on but also keeps you in check when you start slipping into procrastination. That's the magic of *accountability partners*. Having someone alongside you can make a world of difference in staying committed to your goals. This partnership offers mutual motivation, where both of you push each other to stay on track. You're not just working toward your own goals; you're supporting your partner's goals, too. This support boosts your commitment because it's much harder to slack off when you know someone else is counting on you. You find yourself more dedicated, knowing that you're not alone in the struggle against procrastination.

Let's first talk about choosing the right accountability partner. You want someone who shares a similar work ethic and aligns with your goals. It's about finding someone who gets it, who understands what you're working toward, and who won't let you off the hook easily. You need someone who is trustworthy and reliable. You need to know that when you agree to a check-in, they'll be there, ready to talk about progress and challenges. It's a two-way street where you both agree to be dependable, and this creates a foundation of trust. This reliability ensures that both of you stay committed, knowing you can rely on each other to show up and give support.

But once you have your accountability partner, how do you make it work? Regular check-in meetings are a great way to start. Set a schedule that works for both of you, maybe once a week or every few days, to go over what you've done and what still needs to be done. These meetings can be in person or virtual, whatever works best for you. Sharing progress reports during these check-ins can be a great source of motivation. Seeing what your partner has achieved can inspire you to push harder. It's not about competition; it's about using each other's progress to fuel your own motivation. These regular updates keep you both accountable and focused.

A successful partnership has to have support on each side. This means both of you benefit equally. Encourage each other by providing feedback and celebrating small victories. When one of you reaches a milestone, take a moment to acknowledge it, whether it's a quick text of encouragement or a high-five in person. Having a goal-setting session together can also be helpful. Take time to sit down and map out your goals together, offering input and support. This collaboration ensures that you feel invested in each other's success. It's not just about having someone to keep you accountable; it's about creating a supportive environment where you can both be your best.

Accountability partnerships help you stay on track and teach you valuable lessons in teamwork and communication. You learn how to give constructive feedback and how to accept it graciously. This skill is invaluable, not just in school but in life. The partnership becomes a safe space where you can express challenges and celebrate successes without judgment. It's a unique bond that goes beyond the typical friendship because it is rooted in a shared commitment to growth and improvement. You're not just friends; you're allies in the fight against procrastination, pushing each other to reach new heights.

FROM PROCRASTINATOR TO PLANNER: TRANSFORMING YOUR APPROACH

Switching from a procrastinator to a planner doesn't happen overnight, but the techniques you're learning make it much more achievable. Weekly planning sessions are a great place to start. Think of them as your personal strategy meetings. This time is dedicated to laying out your tasks for the upcoming week. Grab a planner or open a digital calendar and start by jotting down all the things you need to accomplish. List everything—from homework assignments to club meetings. This overview helps you see the big picture and manage your time effectively. You're not just writing tasks down; you're mapping out how and when you'll tackle each one. The goal is to transform chaos into order, giving you a clear path forward.

Creating detailed action plans is another powerful tool in your planning arsenal. Instead of looking at a task as a whole, break it down into smaller steps. For example, if you have a science project due, outline each phase from research to final presentation. Assign time frames to each step to ensure you stay on track. This detailed approach makes tasks less overwhelming and provides a sense of accomplishment as you tick off each step. With a clear plan, you're less likely to fall into the trap of procrastination because you know exactly what needs to be done and when.

Structure can reduce uncertainty and procrastination. Try using templates and planners to give your planning process the consistency it needs. Templates offer a framework that guides your thinking and helps you focus on what's important. Whether you prefer digital apps or a good old-fashioned paper planner, having a consistent system means you won't miss anything. A routine can further enhance this structure. Start each day by reviewing your planner and setting intentions. Consistent routines create a rhythm in your life, helping you transition smoothly from one task to the next. This predictability is comforting and keeps procrastination at bay because you're not constantly deciding what to do next.

Let's take it up a notch and include *reflective planning*. Reflective planning takes your strategy to the next level by encouraging you to learn from past experiences. Spend some time each week analyzing what worked and what didn't. Did you underestimate the time needed for a project? Did a particular task take longer because of unexpected challenges? These questions help you understand your planning habits and make necessary adjustments. It's about evolving your strategy to meet your needs. Based on your reflections, tweak your plans to avoid similar problems in the future. This ongoing process of reflecting and adjusting turns planning into a useful tool for self-improvement.

There are a lot of tools and resources out there, so you can find one that fits your unique style. Digital planning apps like Notion or Trello offer flexibility and can sync across devices, keeping your plans accessible anywhere. These apps often include features like reminders and collaborative options, which can be incredibly helpful if you're working on group projects. If you'd rather have something you can hold in your hands, printable planning templates can be a great option. These let you customize your planning process, adding a personal touch that can make planning more fun. The key is to find tools that you like.

MINDFUL MOMENTS: USING MINDFULNESS TO COMBAT DELAY

Have you ever taken a few minutes out of your day to just *be*? Imagine sitting quietly, focusing on the rhythm of your breath, each inhale and exhale connecting you to the present moment. This is mindfulness, a practice that can change how you approach tasks and manage procrastination. Mindfulness helps by anchoring you in the now, cutting through the noise of distractions and future worries.

Mindful breathing exercises are a great starting point. Here's a simple exercise you can try right now: Find a quiet spot, close your eyes, and take deep breaths, paying attention to how the air moves in and out.

This simple exercise can calm your mind, bringing clarity and focus to whatever you're doing.

Similarly, *body scan meditations* guide you to notice sensations throughout your body, promoting relaxation and awareness. All you have to do is this: Picture yourself lying down, scanning from your toes to your head, acknowledging any tension, and releasing it. These practices build a foundation for tackling tasks with a clear and present mindset, reducing the urge to put them off.

Mindfulness isn't just about relaxation; it's a powerful tool for emotional regulation, which can help you deal with procrastination. When you're stressed, it's easy to want to avoid. Mindfulness gives you techniques to manage these feelings, helping you cultivate patience and acceptance. Instead of reacting impulsively to stress, mindfulness teaches you to pay attention to your feelings without judging them. This awareness allows you to respond thoughtfully, choosing actions that align with your goals. Imagine facing a challenging assignment. Stress might make you want to put it off, but with mindfulness, you recognize the stress, breathe through it, and focus on the task at hand. This approach not only reduces anxiety but also builds resilience, making it easier to face challenges head-on.

Like many of the other tools we've talked about, consistency makes mindfulness more powerful. So, like any skill, mindfulness requires regular practice. Consider starting with a daily routine by making time for mindfulness in the morning. Spend a few minutes each day practicing mindful breathing or meditation. This will set the tone for a focused and productive day. As you become more comfortable, bring mindfulness into daily activities. When you eat, pay attention to the flavors and textures. When you're walking, notice the sensations in your feet. This consistent practice strengthens your ability to remain present, making it harder for procrastination to take hold. Over time, mindfulness can become a natural part of your routine, enhancing your focus and reducing the desire to delay.

Mindful goal setting is another strategy to combat procrastination. By using mindfulness, you set clear and intentional goals, focusing on what truly matters. Begin with mindful visualization, where you picture completing your goals and the steps needed to get there. This visualization helps you clarify your intentions, ensuring your goals align with your values. Setting intentions with clarity and focus adds depth to your objectives, making them more meaningful and motivating. Procrastination loses its grip when you're clear about what you want and why. Setting mindful goals grounds you in the present, connecting your daily actions to your broader goals. Each step forward becomes a conscious choice, reinforcing your commitment to achieving your aims.

As we wrap up this chapter, reflect on how mindfulness can reshape your approach to tasks and goals. By fostering present-moment awareness, you equip yourself with the tools to face procrastination with confidence. This chapter has provided you with strategies to manage your time, emotions, and goals effectively. As you move forward, remember that these skills not only help you overcome procrastination but also pave the way for personal growth and success. With these tools, you're ready to tackle whatever comes next, building a foundation for a more focused and intentional future. Now, let's explore how these skills can further enhance your decision-making abilities, setting the stage for empowered choices in the next chapter.

UNLOCK THE POWER OF GIVING BACK

Make a Difference with Your Review

"The best way to find yourself is to lose yourself in the service of others."

— MAHATMA GANDHI

When we give without expecting anything back, it makes us feel good and helps others at the same time. Let's work together to make a difference!

Would you like to help other teens just like you who want to get organized, stay focused, and reach their goals but don't know where to start?

My goal with *Executive Functioning Skills for Teens: From Stress to Success* is to make learning these skills easy and enjoyable for everyone.

But to spread the word and help even more people, I need your support.

Most readers choose their books based on reviews. So, by sharing your experience, you'll be helping someone else take the first step toward getting organized and becoming more confident.

Your review could help...

- one more student finally feel on top of schoolwork.
- one more teen build confidence.
- one more person stop procrastinating and start succeeding.
- one more reader reach their goals.

If you'd like to make a difference, simply scan the QR code below and leave a review:

https://amzn.to/3P7Nk99

Thank you from the bottom of my heart for helping others succeed!

Alexander Wealth

5

DEVELOPING DECISION-MAKING SKILLS

Making decisions can be hard! Imagine you're at an ice cream shop, staring at an overwhelming board of flavors. Should you go for your usual classic chocolate or be more adventurous with something like raspberry cheesecake? This decision might not seem super important, but it's practice for the bigger choices life will throw your way. From picking classes for next semester to deciding on a college or a career, making decisions is a skill that can shape your future. And just like we've seen with all the other skills, it takes practice and the right tools to get it right. This chapter will introduce you to decision-making methods that can help you weigh options and make choices confidently.

Let's start by looking at three of the most popular methods:

- The first tool in your decision-making kit is the classic pros and cons List. It's as simple as it sounds: List the advantages and disadvantages of each option you're considering. This helps you visualize the good and the bad, making the decision clearer.

- Next up is the SWOT analysis, which stands for strengths, weaknesses, opportunities, and threats. This framework is great for more significant decisions, like choosing between two schools or deciding whether to join a new club. By identifying what you're good at (strengths), what might be challenging (weaknesses), what benefits the decision might bring (opportunities), and what obstacles you might face (threats), you better understand your options.
- Finally, there's the decision matrix, which is a bit like creating a scoring system for your choices. You list your options and the factors that matter most, then score each option based on how well it meets those factors. This method is super handy for making smart decisions based on specific information.

Using these methods might sound complicated at first, but breaking it down into steps makes it more simple. Start by identifying your decision criteria. What's important to you when making this choice? If you're deciding on a summer job, your criteria might include pay, location, and work hours. Once you know what matters, weigh the potential outcomes. For example, a job that pays more but is farther away might cost you more in travel time and money, while a closer job could free up time for friends and family. Think about each option carefully, using a decision-making method to organize your thoughts. This process helps clarify your goals and keeps emotions out of it, ensuring your decisions line up with your true priorities.

These decision-making tools have tons of benefits. They guide you in organizing your thoughts, reducing the chaos that often comes when you have a lot of options. By laying everything out clearly, you can see patterns and potential problems you might have missed. This clarity leads to better-informed decisions and fewer regrets. Additionally, these tools help cut through emotional biases that can cloud your judgment. It's easy to be swayed by what feels right in the moment, but by using a structured approach, you ensure your decisions are grounded in logic and reason.

Remember that these frameworks are not one-size-fits-all. Personalizing them to suit your style is key. Incorporating your personal values into the decision-making process ensures your choices reflect who you are and what you stand for. Adjust the decision criteria based on what is important to you. This ensures the decision-making process feels authentic and aligned with your goals.

INTERACTIVE ELEMENT: DECISION-MAKING WORKSHEET

This exercise helps you apply what you've learned and see the benefits of these frameworks in action. To help you get started:

1. Create a decision-making worksheet.
2. List a decision you're facing, then outline a pros and cons List, a SWOT analysis, and a decision matrix for it.
3. Fill it out with your decision criteria and scores.
4. Reflect on the insights you gain and how they influence your choice.

PRACTICING SAFE DECISION-MAKING: SIMULATIONS AND SCENARIOS

Have you ever seen a play or been to the theater? Picture being part of a school production or drama club where you get to play different roles in various scenes. This is acting, of course, but you can also see it as practicing decision-making in a safe space without real-world consequences. Role-playing exercises are powerful tools for sharpening your decision-making skills. They allow you to step into different scenarios, explore various outcomes, and see the effects of your choices. Whether you're pretending to be a student council president or navigating a tricky friendship situation, these exercises help you experiment and learn without the fear of making a wrong choice that impacts your real life. Interactive decision-making games are another cool way to practice. They challenge you to think on your feet, adapt to changing circumstances, and make quick decisions, all within a fun and controlled environment.

Think about having to choose between extracurricular activities. You love playing soccer, but the drama club also calls to you. How do you decide which one to join? In a simulation, you might list out what each activity offers—soccer might improve your teamwork skills and physical fitness, while drama could boost your confidence and creativity. You weigh these factors, consider your schedule, and decide which fits best with your interests and goals. It's a chance to practice prioritizing and balancing your commitments, skills that will benefit you in real life. What about something else, like a disagreement with a friend? You can explore different ways to handle the situation through role-playing. You might choose to have a direct conversation, compromise, or get advice from a trusted adult. These scenarios help you practice empathy and communication, which are essential for good decision-making.

Once you practice these simulations, take some time to analyze the decisions you made. Much like the reflective planning we talked about in the last chapter, reflective debriefing sessions allow you to step back and take a look at what happened. Did the choice you made turn out how you wanted? If not, why? Identifying lessons learned from each exercise helps you understand what worked, what didn't, and how you can improve. Reflective debriefing isn't about criticizing yourself; it's about learning more for your future decisions. By thinking about your choices, you get a deeper understanding of your decision-making process. This helps you see patterns in your thinking and find areas where you might need to make changes.

Building confidence in decision-making takes continuous practice. Think about setting up weekly decision-making challenges where you tackle different scenarios and gradually make them harder. This practice keeps your skills sharp and prepares you for real-life situations. You can also practice with a group. Other people can introduce diverse perspectives and collaborative problem-solving. Working with others lets you see how different people approach the same decision, offering new insights and strategies you might not have considered.

Interactive Element: Decision-Making Challenge

Create a weekly decision-making challenge with friends or family. Here's what to do:

1. Choose a scenario, like planning a group outing or resolving a fictional conflict.
2. Discuss different solutions, role-play various outcomes, and debrief afterward.
3. Reflect on what each of you learned and how you can apply these insights to real-life decisions.

This exercise strengthens your decision-making skills and creates a supportive environment where you can learn from each other's experiences.

TRUSTING YOUR GUT: WHEN TO LISTEN TO INTUITION

Has there ever been a time when you just knew something without needing to think it through? That feeling, that gut instinct, is your *intuition* at work. While sometimes it can seem mysterious, intuition can actually be a valuable tool in decision-making—especially when you need to make quick decisions or when you don't have all the information. Picture yourself in a basketball game, the clock ticking down, and you have to make a pass. You don't have time to analyze every possibility; you trust your gut, going with the teammate who's most likely to score. In scenarios like these, intuition can guide you to make decisions quickly and confidently.

But how do you get better at trusting your gut? Developing intuitive skills isn't about guessing. It involves training your mind to recognize patterns and signals that your subconscious picks up. Practicing mindfulness can help enhance your intuition. Mindfulness involves being present in the moment, which sharpens your awareness and helps you pick up on subtle cues. By paying attention to your surroundings and your own feelings, you become more attuned to your instincts. Reflecting on past intuitive decisions can also help. Think about times when you trusted your gut, and it turned out well. What were the signs that led you to that decision? By reflecting, you learn to recognize those signals more easily in the future.

Balancing intuition with reason is crucial. While your gut can guide you in certain situations, relying solely on intuition can sometimes lead to impulsive choices. Recognizing intuitive signals is the first step. Maybe it's a feeling of excitement or a sense of calm when you think of an option. Once you've identified these signals, think about them logically. Ask yourself if the choice aligns with your goals and if the potential outcomes make sense. This combination of intuition and reason ensures that your decisions are both thoughtful and aligned with your instincts.

Building confidence in your intuition comes from seeing it succeed. Think of successful entrepreneurs who trusted their instincts to innovate and create something new. Their stories show how intuition can lead to breakthroughs when combined with a strategic approach. Personal stories from relatable figures can also inspire trust in your gut. Maybe a family member made a life-changing decision by following their intuition, which worked out for the best. These examples can reassure you that intuition is a skill worth nurturing.

Textual Element: Reflection Section

You can make more confident and well-rounded choices by understanding when and how to listen to your intuition. Reflect on a decision where you relied on your intuition, and ask yourself:

1. What were the circumstances, and how did it feel to trust your gut?
2. Did the outcome align with your expectations?
3. Write about the signs that guided you and what you learned from the experience.

This reflection helps reinforce your intuitive skills, making it easier to trust them in future decisions.

LEARNING FROM MISTAKES: TURNING FAILURES INTO LEARNING OPPORTUNITIES

Picture this: You studied hard for a math test, but you get your grade back and realize you did much worse than you thought you would. What if instead of seeing it as a setback, you see it as a stepping stone? Mistakes aren't roadblocks; they're signs pointing out what needs work. Think back to the growth mindset we talked about earlier in the book. Encouraging a growth mindset means viewing mistakes as opportunities for growth, not failures. When you learn to see failures as feedback, you stop feeling defeated and start being motivated to improve. Remember: This mindset isn't about ignoring mistakes but embracing them as part of the learning process. Think of each mistake as a clue in a mystery you're solving—each one brings you closer to the answer.

To really gain from mistakes, a simple game of pretend can be helpful. Imagine you're a detective studying what went wrong. Like a detective examining a case, you'll want to look back and identify the factors that led to the mistake. Was it a lack of preparation, a misunderstanding, or maybe just a bad day? Once you know what went wrong, think about what else you could have done. It's like replaying a video game level where you keep dying at the same spot. You look at your approach, tweak your strategy, and try again until you get through it. By doing this, you're not just learning what went wrong; you're figuring out how to get it right next time.

This process of learning and changing builds *resilience*, the ability to face challenges and adjust to them. Imagine resilience as a muscle that gets stronger with use. Each time you face a setback and bounce back, you strengthen that muscle. Developing coping strategies, or things you can do when you're struggling, helps you manage the emotions that come with failure, like frustration or disappointment. Maybe it's taking a walk to clear your head or talking it out with a friend. Once you've dealt with the emotions, it's time to set new goals. These goals aren't just about fixing what went wrong but moving forward with a fresh perspective. They give you a sense of direction and purpose, turning a negative experience into a positive drive for improvement.

Inspirational success stories can serve as powerful motivators. Take inventors like Thomas Edison, who famously failed thousands of times before perfecting the light bulb. Each failure taught him something new, ultimately leading to his success. Or think of entrepreneurs like Steve Jobs, whose early career setbacks didn't stop him from revolutionizing technology. These stories show that failure isn't the end; it's part of the process. Closer to home, you might know peers who've faced challenges, like a friend who didn't make the team on their first try but practiced harder and made it the next season. Personal stories are equally valuable and offer relatable examples of resilience and determination.

So, instead of fearing failure, embrace it as part of your personal development. Mistakes can be some of your best teachers. It's not about aiming for perfection but striving for progress. Next time you have a setback, remember that it's an opportunity to learn something new, refine your skills, and come back stronger. Mistakes are simply proof that you're trying, and trying is how you grow.

PEER INFLUENCE: MAKING DECISIONS INDEPENDENTLY

Have you ever had more than one person trying to tell you what to do? Imagine standing at a crossroads, surrounded by friends all eagerly voicing their opinions. "Go this way!" "No, go that way!" It's easy to get caught up in what your peers think, especially with so much pressure to conform—not to mention a heavy dose of FOMO. Peer pressure can heavily sway your decision-making, often pushing you toward choices that go along with the group rather than your values. This isn't always negative—sometimes, your peers can inspire you to try new things or push your boundaries in a positive way. However, you still need to be able to make decisions on your own. It's about finding the balance between listening to others and staying true to yourself.

When considering peer advice, it's essential to consider the source and intent. Ask yourself: Who is giving this advice, and why? Are they genuinely looking out for your best interests, or is there another motive at play? Balancing peer input with your personal values can be challenging, but it's essential for making decisions that you won't regret. It helps to weigh the advice against what you know to be true about yourself. If a friend suggests skipping a study session for a party, think about how that aligns with your academic goals. Does their idea support your priorities, or is it a distraction from them? By carefully considering this, you can get valuable insights from your peers while staying aligned with your values.

Developing independent thinking starts with knowing yourself well. Journaling about your personal values and goals can be a powerful tool in this process. When you take the time to write down what's important to you, it becomes easier to make decisions that align with your path. Reflecting on these values regularly helps ground your decisions, especially when group dynamics come into play. Practicing self-reflection before making group decisions is another way to ensure your choices are your own. Before agreeing to something, take a moment to pause and ask yourself if this is what you truly want. This practice builds a habit of looking inside yourself, allowing you to make better decisions.

Being assertive, or voicing your opinion, is a critical skill in making independent decisions. It's about expressing your needs and desires clearly without being swayed by others. Role-playing assertive communication can help you practice this skill. Imagine a situation where you need to say no to a friend. Practicing how to explain your reasoning assertively yet respectfully prepares you for real-life scenarios. Setting personal boundaries is also key. Boundaries act as guidelines that define what you are comfortable with and what you are not willing to compromise on. They protect your time, energy, and values, allowing you to make decisions that reflect your true self.

Building these skills doesn't mean isolating yourself from others or ignoring valuable advice. It's about finding that sweet spot where you can listen to your peers, consider their perspectives, and still make choices that feel right for you. Doing this strengthens your ability to navigate peer influence confidently, ensuring that your decisions reflect who you are and who you aspire to be.

BUILDING CONFIDENCE IN YOUR CHOICES

Let's move on to a different aspect of decision-making: confidence. Imagine standing on the edge of a diving board, looking down at the pool below. The water seems inviting, but it's confidence that pushes you to leap. Confidence in decision-making works just like that. It's the belief in your decision that guides you past thinking about your options to actually taking action. Confidence boosts your ability to follow through on decisions and reduces the second-guessing that can paralyze you. When you're sure of your choice, you're more likely to stick with it, even when challenges come up. This assurance not only influences how successful your outcomes are but also how you feel about the decisions you make. It's the difference between hesitating at the edge and diving in with a splash.

Building confidence starts with small steps. Positive affirmations are a simple yet powerful tool. They're like pep talks for your brain, reminding you of your strengths and abilities. Start your day by telling yourself, "I am capable of making the right choices," or "I trust my instincts." These affirmations might initially feel awkward, but they reinforce a positive mindset that boosts your confidence over time. Alongside affirmations, try setting and achieving small goals. Each goal you accomplish, no matter how tiny, is a victory that builds your confidence. Whether it's completing a chapter in a book or learning a new skill, these successes build on each other, strengthening your belief in your ability to make decisions.

Positive self-talk is another way to reinforce confidence. It's about being your own cheerleader and silencing the inner critic. Developing a personal mantra can help. This short, powerful phrase acts as a mental reset button, refocusing your thoughts when doubt creeps in. Maybe it's something like "I've got this" or "Keep pushing forward." Whenever negative thoughts start to swirl, challenge them. Ask yourself if these thoughts are based on facts or just fears. Replace them with your mantra, reminding yourself of your capabilities and past successes. This shift in mindset can transform how you approach decisions, making you more confident and decisive.

Stories of individuals overcoming doubt to make confident decisions can be inspiring here, too. Think about an athlete who battles performance anxiety before every game. Through practice and mental conditioning, they learn to trust their training and perform with confidence, turning nerves into focus. Or imagine a student leader making difficult decisions within a school club. By listening to input, weighing options, and trusting their judgment, they lead their team to success. These stories show how confidence in decision-making can lead to positive outcomes, even in the face of uncertainty.

Confidence in your choices doesn't come from never making mistakes but from learning to trust yourself and your process. It's about having faith in your ability to make informed decisions and adapt when necessary. With each decision you make, you build a foundation of experience and self-assurance. This confidence moves you forward, helping you navigate life's uncertainties. Remember, every choice is an opportunity to learn and grow. So, take that leap, trust in your ability to swim, and embrace the journey ahead.

As we wrap up this chapter on decision-making, consider how each skill you've learned can be a tool in your toolbox. From decision-making methods and intuition to resilience and confidence, these skills equip you to tackle decisions successfully. Now, let's explore how emotional regulation and resilience play a role in mastering executive functioning skills.

6

EMOTIONAL REGULATION AND RESILIENCE

For this next chapter, let's imagine you're at a theme park, and you're about to ride the tallest roller coaster. Your heart is pounding, your palms are sweaty, and you can't decide if you're excited or terrified. This mix of emotions is a lot like the ups and downs of life, and knowing how to handle those feelings is key to keeping your cool. Welcome to the world of emotional regulation and resilience, where we'll explore how to recognize your emotions and responses and guide you in bouncing back from life's inevitable twists and turns. This chapter is all about understanding what makes you tick emotionally and how you can use that knowledge to handle tough situations.

RECOGNIZING EMOTIONAL TRIGGERS AND RESPONSES

Let's start with emotional triggers. We've talked about triggers a few times already: They are situations or events that can cause strong reactions. Sometimes, it happens without you even realizing it. For a lot of teens, social media can be a big trigger. Scrolling through endless posts of perfect vacations or flawless selfies might make you feel like you're not measuring up. This comparison game can make you feel jealous or like you're not enough. Academic stress is another common trigger. Whether it's the pressure of a test coming up or the fear of not meeting expectations, school can sometimes feel overwhelming. Then, there's peer conflict—disagreements with friends or feeling left out can stir up emotions like anger, sadness, or anxiety. Recognizing these triggers is the first step in managing them. When you know what sets you off, you can start taking control of how you respond.

Emotions can show up in both physical and mental ways. Imagine you're about to give a presentation in class. Your heart might race, your hands could shake, and your stomach might feel like it's doing flips. These physical responses are your body's way of reacting to stress or excitement. Mentally, you might find yourself spiraling into negative thoughts—worrying about what others think or being afraid that you'll mess up. These thought patterns can cloud your judgment and make a situation seem worse than it is. But you can start to manage your responses by becoming aware of how your body and mind react.

Self-reflection is a powerful tool for building awareness of your emotions. One way to start is by keeping an emotion diary. It's pretty simple: Each day, jot down situations that triggered strong emotions and note your reactions. Think about what you felt and why. Over time, this can help you find patterns in your emotional responses. Maybe you notice that you often feel anxious before math tests or frustrated when plans with friends fall through. Understanding these patterns allows you to anticipate and prepare for similar situations in the future. It's like having a map to navigate your feelings, helping you stay grounded even when emotions run high.

As you explore these patterns, pay attention to anything that comes up a lot, as they often reveal the root causes of your emotional responses. Is there a specific class or social setting that consistently makes you feel uneasy? Think about how intense the emotion was and how long it lasted. Was your reaction quick, or did it hang around and affect your whole day? Thinking back like this enhances your emotional intelligence and equips you to handle emotions with more confidence.

Interactive Element: Emotion Diary Exercise

Create your own emotion diary. Here's what to do:

1. Each day for a week, write about moments that triggered strong emotions.
2. Include what happened, how you felt physically and mentally, and why you think you reacted the way you did.
3. At the end of the week, review your entries to look for patterns. Are there common triggers? How did your responses vary?
4. Use these insights to develop strategies for managing your emotions in future situations.

This exercise not only helps you understand your emotions but also empowers you to take steps to regulate how you respond.

Recognizing your emotional triggers and understanding your responses help you navigate life's roller coasters. By identifying what sets you off and reflecting on your reactions, you gain the power to manage your emotions rather than letting them manage you.

STRESS-REDUCTION TECHNIQUES FOR EVERYDAY LIFE

Here's another thought experiment: Imagine that your mind is a glass of water. Each drop of stress adds to the glass, and sometimes, it feels like it's about to overflow. But what if you could pour some of that water out? That's where stress-reduction techniques come in. Let's look at some of them:

One simple method is deep breathing exercises. It might sound basic, but taking a few slow, deep breaths can work wonders for calming your nerves. When you're stressed, your breathing becomes shallow and quick, which can make anxiety worse. By focusing on slow, deep breaths, you signal your body to relax. Try inhaling deeply through your nose, holding it for a few seconds, and then slowly exhaling through your mouth. Do this a few times, and you'll likely notice a difference in how you feel.

Another technique is progressive muscle relaxation. Basically, this means tensing and then relaxing different muscle groups. This can help release physical tension that's built up from stress. Start with your toes, tense them for a few seconds, then let go. Work your way up through your body—calves, thighs, abdomen, arms, and so on. This helps you become more aware of where you hold tension and teaches you how to relax those areas. It's like giving your muscles a mini-vacation, allowing them to unwind and reset.

Physical activity is another powerful stress-buster. When you move your body, whether through exercise, sports, or dance, you release endorphins, those feel-good chemicals that boost your mood. Regular exercise routines, even just a 20-minute walk or a quick dance session, can reduce stress. Sports or dance provides a physical outlet for stress and gives you a chance to focus on something enjoyable and challenging. It's a break from the daily grind, allowing you to return to your tasks with a clearer mind.

In Chapter 2, we talked a lot about managing your time. Effective time management also plays an important role in reducing stress. When you prioritize tasks and set realistic deadlines, you avoid the last-minute rush that can send stress levels soaring. Use the skills you've learned to break down big projects into smaller, manageable parts and tackle them one step at a time. This makes tasks feel less overwhelming and gives you a sense of accomplishment as you complete each part. Having a plan in place helps you stay organized and focused and prevents the chaos that often leads to stress.

Creating a personal relaxation space is another way to keep stress at bay. Think of it as your sanctuary, a place where you can unwind and recharge. It doesn't have to be over the top. A cozy corner in your room with a comfortable chair, soft lighting, and a few calming scents like lavender can do the trick. These things create a soothing environment that invites relaxation. When you need a break, go to this space to read, meditate, or simply breathe. It's a way to step back from the hustle and bustle and give yourself permission to relax and recharge.

Stress is a part of life, but it doesn't have to control you. You can manage stress more effectively by using these stress-reduction techniques. These strategies not only help you feel better in the moment but also build resilience, equipping you to handle future challenges with greater ease.

As you explore these techniques, remember that it's about finding what works best for you. Experiment with different methods and see how they fit into your life. Whether it's through movement, relaxation, or time management, each step you take is a step toward a healthier, happier you.

BUILDING A RESILIENCE TOOLKIT: STRATEGIES FOR BOUNCING BACK

We've talked about resilience before, so you might not be surprised that being resilient helps you manage stress, too. Imagine resilience as your personal shield. It keeps you steady when life throws curveballs. Whether it's a disappointing grade or losing someone close, resilience helps you get back on your feet. You could also think of it like a rubber band that stretches but never breaks. When faced with academic setbacks, like bombed tests or overwhelming workloads, resilience encourages you to try again. It's the voice that says, "You've got this," even when the going gets tough. Dealing with personal loss, whether it's a friendship that fades or a more profound loss, resilience allows you to process your emotions and find a path forward. It's about learning to weather the storm and come out stronger, ready to take on whatever comes next.

Building resilience isn't just about having a positive attitude; it's about actively developing skills that help you adapt to changes. One way to enhance resilience is through problem-solving exercises. These activities challenge you to think critically and find solutions to complex issues. You might try completing a puzzle or engaging in brain-teasers that require you to think outside the box. These exercises train your brain to stay flexible and open to new approaches. Role-playing scenarios are another great tool. By putting yourself in hypothetical situations, like having a conflict with a friend or handling another stressful event, you practice responding calmly and thoughtfully. These pretend situations prepare you for real-life challenges, allowing you to test your resilience in a safe space.

Support networks can also build your resilience. Surrounding yourself with people who care can make all the difference. Family and friends provide a safety net, offering comfort and encouragement when you need it most. They're the ones who cheer you on when you succeed and pick you up when you stumble. Mentors and teachers also contribute to your resilience. They bring wisdom and guidance, helping you see challenges as opportunities for growth. Having a solid support system reminds you that you're not alone and that it's okay to lean on others when times get tough.

That positive mindset we've talked about is another key piece of resilience. It's not about ignoring the negative but focusing on the good things in life. Practicing gratitude can change your perspective, highlighting the silver linings even on cloudy days. Try this: Start by noting three things you're grateful for each day, whether it's a nice thing a friend said or a funny meme that made you laugh. This practice can boost your mood and build a more positive outlook. Focusing on strengths is important, too. Recognize what you're good at and find ways to use those talents. Whether it's your creativity, problem-solving skills, or ability to connect with others, these strengths are your toolkit for resilience.

Developing resilience takes time and practice, but it's worth it. With a resilient mindset, you face challenges with confidence, knowing that setbacks are just stepping stones on your path. Resilience helps you navigate life's ups and downs with grace, empowering you to keep moving forward, no matter what.

THE POWER OF SELF-COMPASSION: BEING KIND TO YOURSELF

We all struggle at times. Sometimes, it's easier to think of how we would help a friend instead of how to help ourselves. So, imagine you're talking to a friend who's feeling down because they didn't do well on a test. What would you say to them? Most likely, you'd encourage them, remind them of their strengths, and tell them that one setback doesn't mean they're not capable of great things. Now, imagine saying the same things to yourself. That's *self-compassion*. It's about treating yourself with the same kindness and understanding you'd give to someone you care about. Instead of being your harshest critic, self-compassion allows you to be your best ally. By saying no thanks to self-criticism, you open the door to emotional recovery. It's like a soothing balm for your spirit, helping you bounce back from disappointments with greater resilience. When you practice self-compassion, you create a safe space within yourself to grow and heal rather than getting stuck in a cycle of negativity.

You can practice self-compassion in your daily life through simple acts. Start with self-compassionate self-talk. When you catch yourself in a spiral of negative thoughts, pause and reframe those thoughts kindly. Instead of saying, "I messed up," try, "It's okay to make mistakes, and I can learn from this." This shift in language can make a huge difference in how you perceive yourself and your experiences. Another practice is forgiving yourself. We often hold ourselves to impossibly high standards, and when we fall short, we can be unforgiving. Acknowledge that it's human to make mistakes, and allow yourself the grace to move past those moments. Forgiveness isn't about excusing mistakes but understanding that they are how we learn.

Just like it does in many of the other skills we're learning about, self-reflection plays a key role in self-compassion. Reflective journaling can be incredibly useful here, too. Take some time to write about your day, focusing on moments when you were too hard on yourself. Ask yourself why you reacted that way and think about how you could handle similar situations with more kindness. Accepting past failures as learning opportunities is another powerful aspect of self-reflection. Everyone stumbles, but as we know from developing a growth mindset, each stumble is a stepping stone to something greater. By embracing your imperfections, you free yourself from the fear of making mistakes and allow yourself to grow. It's about seeing the bigger picture and recognizing that every experience, good or bad, is part of your development.

Let's look at some real-life examples of self-compassion in action: Take an athlete who's suddenly not doing well. Instead of beating themselves up, they embrace self-compassion by focusing on what they can control and setting small, achievable goals to rebuild their confidence. With time and kindness toward themselves, they find their rhythm again, proving that self-compassion is a vital part of resilience. Or consider a student who faced academic setbacks. Rather than dwelling on their grades, they used self-compassion to acknowledge their efforts, celebrate progress, and seek support when needed. By doing so, they not only improved academically but also developed a healthier relationship with themselves, understanding that their worth isn't tied to a report card.

These stories highlight the power of self-compassion. By being kinder to yourself, you pave the way for emotional healing and personal growth. You learn to navigate challenges with courage and grace, knowing that you have a friend within who believes in your potential. Self-compassion doesn't happen overnight; it's a lifelong practice that enriches your emotional intelligence and allows you to thrive in every aspect of your life.

MINDFULNESS PRACTICES FOR EMOTIONAL BALANCE

At some point, we've all found ourselves daydreaming during class or zoning out while someone's talking. It happens, and that's where mindfulness comes in. As we know now, mindfulness is all about being present, really focusing on the here and now. It's like turning the volume up on your senses and tuning out the noise that distracts you. When you practice mindfulness, you can reduce stress and find emotional balance. Imagine having a superpower that lets you control your reactions and stay calm even when things get crazy. That's what mindfulness can do for you. It helps you notice your thoughts and feelings without getting swept away by them. This kind of awareness can make a huge difference, especially when life feels overwhelming.

One of the simplest ways to practice mindfulness is through mindful breathing exercises. Here's one simple way you can be mindful today:

1. Start by finding a quiet spot where you won't be disturbed.
2. Sit comfortably and close your eyes if you're okay with it.
3. Take a deep breath in through your nose, letting your chest and belly expand.
4. Hold it for a moment, then slowly exhale through your mouth.
5. Pay attention to how the air feels entering and leaving your body as you breathe. Notice the rise and fall of your chest.
6. If your mind starts to wander, gently bring your focus back to your breath.

This exercise isn't about emptying your mind but about being aware of the present moment. Even a few minutes of mindful breathing each day can help you feel more grounded and less stressed.

Another powerful technique is *body scan meditation*. It isn't difficult; it involves focusing on different parts of your body, one at a time, and noticing any sensations without judgment. Try this:

1. Find a comfortable position, either lying down or sitting.
2. Close your eyes and take a few deep breaths to relax.
3. Then, start by bringing your attention to your toes. Notice how they feel. Are they warm, cold, tense, or relaxed?
4. Gradually move your focus up through your body—feet, legs, abdomen, chest, arms, and finally, your head.
5. As you scan each area, release any tension you find.

This practice can help you become more in tune with your body and reduce physical stress.

Incorporating mindfulness into daily life doesn't have to be a big deal. It's about making small changes that fit into your routine. Take mindful eating, for example. Instead of scarfing down your lunch while scrolling through your phone, try focusing on each bite. Notice the textures and flavors. Chew slowly and savor your food. This simple shift can turn a rushed meal into a moment of calm. Walking meditation is another way to practice mindfulness on the go. As you walk, pay attention to the sensation of your feet touching the ground. Be aware of your surroundings—the sights, sounds, and smells. These practices help you stay present and connected to the world around you.

If you want some extra help and motivation, mindfulness apps like Calm and Headspace are the way to go. These apps provide guided meditations tailored to different needs, whether you want to reduce anxiety, improve focus, or sleep better. Headspace is great for beginners. It offers short, easy-to-follow sessions that fit into even the busiest schedules. Calm features a variety of meditations and even sleep stories to help you unwind. These tools can be a fantastic way to start building mindfulness in your life.

Journaling for Emotional Clarity and Growth

Journaling is a tool that can help with so many of the skills we're learning. Think of it as a conversation with yourself. It's a space where you can spill your thoughts and emotions; it helps you make sense of all the chaos inside your head sometimes. Writing things down helps you process complex emotions, like that knot of anxiety before a big test or the mix of excitement and fear when you try something new. By documenting your progress, you can track how you handle these feelings over time. This process not only helps you understand your emotions but also highlights your growth. You'll see how you tackled challenges and came out stronger, offering a clearer picture of who you are and who you're becoming. Journaling acts like a mirror, reflecting your innermost thoughts and helping you understand them better.

There are so many ways to journal; the beauty is finding what works best for you. Free writing is one technique that allows for emotional release. Here, you let your thoughts flow without worrying about grammar or structure. Set a timer for ten minutes, and just write whatever comes to mind. Being unfiltered can be incredibly freeing, letting you vent frustrations or explore dreams without judgment.

On the other hand, structured prompts offer guided reflection, helping you focus on specific aspects of your life. These can be questions like, "What am I grateful for today?" or "What's one thing I learned this week?" Prompts can guide your thoughts, making it easier to dive into more profound reflection.

Consistency is key when it comes to journaling. Setting a regular schedule helps make it a habit. Maybe you write every night before bed, reflecting on the day's events, or perhaps once a week is more your style, offering a broader overview of your experiences. Some people prefer using a traditional journal, feeling the pen glide across paper, while others might choose a digital journal or app, enjoying the convenience and organization. The important thing is to find a rhythm that suits you, ensuring journaling becomes a regular part of your emotional exploration. This consistency turns journaling into a powerful tool for self-discovery and growth.

Let's look at the story of Alex, a high school senior who felt overwhelmed by academic pressure and uncertain about the future. By committing to journaling, Alex found a way to sort through these emotions. Writing allowed Alex to see patterns in stress responses and recognize the small victories along the way. Reflective writing gave him insights into personal strengths and areas for improvement, turning anxiety into a manageable challenge. Through journaling, Alex gained a clearer perspective and developed a sense of empowerment, making him ready to face the future confidently.

Another success story comes from Jamie, who used journaling to help with a complicated friendship. By reflecting on interactions and emotions, Jamie discovered underlying issues and patterns that she hadn't noticed. This awareness led Jamie to approach the friendship with greater empathy and understanding, ultimately strengthening their bond. Journaling provided Jamie with a safe space to process feelings and develop strategies for communication. Journaling helped her change her approach and grow in her personal relationships and self-awareness.

As we wrap up this chapter on emotional regulation and resilience, think of these skills as your toolkit for navigating life's challenges. Recognizing emotional triggers, practicing stress-reduction techniques, and building resilience are all part of the bigger picture of self-improvement. With these tools, you're better equipped to handle whatever comes your way. This sets the stage for the next chapter, where we will explore the exciting world of goal-setting and personal achievement.

7

SETTING AND ACHIEVING GOALS

Imagine you're standing at the edge of a soccer field, the ball at your feet, the goalpost ahead. Every move you make on the field is aimed at one target: the goal. Just like in a soccer game, life is about setting your sights on specific objectives and then taking steps to score. But without a clear aim, it's easy to get lost in the chaos of everyday life. That's where goal-setting comes in. It's your strategy, your game plan for turning dreams into reality. And the best part? You don't need to be a superstar athlete to use it. This chapter is all about making your goals SMART—because a little structure can make all the difference.

Let's dive into the SMART framework. We already know what it stands for: specific, measurable, achievable, relevant, and time-bound. Each piece plays a crucial role in shaping goals that aren't just lofty dreams but real targets you can hit. Let's look at SMART goals a little more in depth:

- Being specific means clearly defining what you want. Instead of saying, "I want to do better in school," try, "I want to improve my math grade from a B to an A by the end of the semester." The more detailed your goal, the easier it is to focus your efforts.
- Measurable goals let you track progress. If your goal is to save money, decide on an exact amount—say $100 by the end of two months. This way, you can see how close you are to your target, which keeps you motivated.
- Achievable goals are realistic. If you're not a morning person, deciding to wake up at 5 a.m. every day to study might not be practical. Instead, aim for something within reach, like starting your study session 30 minutes earlier.
- Relevant goals align with what matters to you. If playing guitar is your passion, setting a goal to practice regularly makes sense.
- Lastly, time-bound means setting a deadline, like preparing for a school play audition in three weeks. Deadlines create a sense of urgency, preventing procrastination and keeping you on track.

Now, let's get into how you craft your own SMART goals. Start by thinking about what truly matters to you. Maybe you want to improve your basketball skills, become more social, or ace your history class. Once you have a broad idea, break it down using the SMART criteria. Let's say your academic goal is to boost your history grade:

1. Make it specific by deciding to focus on improving your essay-writing skills.
2. Measurable might be aiming for a score of 85% or higher on your next essay.
3. Ensure it's achievable by setting aside 30 minutes each day for focused practice.

4. Keep it relevant by tying it to your broader academic aspirations, like getting into a college of your choice.
5. Make it time-bound by setting a deadline, such as achieving this by the end of the current quarter. This structure not only clarifies your path but also makes the end result feel attainable.

The beauty of SMART goals is that they provide clarity and motivation. They take away the unknowns that often cloud goal-setting and give you a clear direction. When you know exactly what you're aiming for and how to get there, so it's easier to stay focused. Each step you take toward your goal is a step in the right direction, which reduces the chances of getting sidetracked. Plus, seeing your progress can be incredibly motivating. Imagine the satisfaction of checking off a completed task or seeing your savings grow week by week. It's these small victories that fuel your journey, making the process as rewarding as the outcome.

Reflecting on past goals can be helpful. Look back at previous goals—what worked and what didn't? Did you set a goal to join a club but never followed through? Maybe it wasn't specific enough, or perhaps it wasn't something you genuinely cared about. Thinking about these successes and challenges can help improve your approach. It's about learning from experience and adjusting your strategies to better fit your changing goals. As you set new goals, keep the SMART framework in mind. It's not just a tool; it's your secret weapon for turning ambitions into achievements!

INTERACTIVE ELEMENT: SMART GOAL WORKSHEET

Create your own SMART goal using this process. Follow these steps:

1. Write down a goal you want to achieve, and then break it down into each component of the SMART framework.

2. Be specific about what you want and how you'll measure success and ensure it's achievable and relevant.
3. Set a deadline to keep yourself accountable.
4. Use this process as a guide to craft goals that are clear and motivating, tailored to your unique aspirations.

This exercise helps solidify the concept and gives you a tangible plan to follow, transforming your goals from ideas into actionable steps.

VISUALIZING SUCCESS: CREATING VISION BOARDS

Have you ever flipped through a magazine and landed on a picture that perfectly captures something you dream of achieving? Maybe it's a picture of a university campus, a professional athlete, or even a serene beach. Now, imagine gathering all these images, quotes, and words that resonate with your goals and aspirations and arranging them in a way that speaks directly to your heart. This is a *vision board*. It's a visual representation of your dreams, and it gives you a daily reminder of what you're working toward. Creating a vision board involves selecting images and words that symbolize where you want to go and who you want to become. The process is both reflective and creative, allowing you to explore what truly matters to you.

The first step in creating a vision board is deciding on a medium. Will you go old-school with a physical board, cutting out images from magazines and arranging them on a corkboard or poster? Or does a digital version appeal to you more, using tools like Pinterest or Canva to compile your dreams in a virtual space? Both have their perks. A physical board offers a hands-on experience and can be a fun art project. In contrast, a digital board allows for easy updates and access from anywhere. Once you've decided, start collecting images and words that resonate with your goals. Perhaps you're drawn to a picture of a bustling city if you're aiming for a career in business or a serene nature scene if peace and balance are what you seek. Arrange these elements by theme or category, creating sections for different aspects of your life, such as career, health, and relationships. The layout should feel meaningful to you, reflecting your aspirations in an inspiring and motivating way.

Visualization is a powerful tool, and creating a vision board has a lot of benefits. By visualizing success, you strengthen your emotional connection to your goals. It's like watching a trailer for a movie you're excited about—it builds anticipation and keeps you engaged. When you visualize your goals, you clarify what you truly want, and this enhances your motivation to pursue them. It's as if your mind starts paving pathways toward achieving what you see. Seeing your dreams in front of you daily reinforces your commitment, reminding you why you're putting in the effort. It can transform a distant dream into a real-life target, making it feel within reach.

A vision board also doesn't have to be a one-time creation. As you grow and your goals shift, your board should evolve with you. Set aside time each month or so to review and update your board. This regular review ensures it remains a true reflection of your current goals and aspirations. Maybe you've achieved a milestone and want to add a new goal, or maybe your interests have shifted, and your board needs a refresh to reflect that change. Adding new elements as goals evolve keeps the board dynamic and relevant, serving as a constant source of inspiration and focus. This process helps you stay connected to your aspirations, ensuring that your vision board continues to motivate and guide you on your path.

BREAKING DOWN BIG GOALS INTO MANAGEABLE STEPS

Let's think again about tackling that mountain of homework. If you stare at the pile as a whole, it can feel like it's towering over you, impossible to climb. That's where breaking down big goals into smaller, manageable tasks comes in. When faced with a big goal, it's easy to feel overwhelmed, almost like you're at the base of a mountain and can't even see the top. But by dissecting your goals into bite-sized pieces, you not only make the task less intimidating but also enhance your focus on what needs to be done right now. It's like turning that mountain into a series of small hills. This approach lets you concentrate on one hill at a time, making the overall task seem much more achievable.

To break down your goals, start by creating detailed task lists. Begin with your primary goal, then brainstorm all the steps required to reach it. Organize these tasks by importance and urgency, ensuring you tackle the most pressing ones first. Imagine you want to improve your grades by the end of the semester. Your task list might include reviewing past assignments, setting up study groups, and meeting with teachers for extra help. Prioritizing these tasks helps streamline your efforts so you're not scattered and wasting energy on less important things. It's all about focusing your resources where they're most needed, ensuring that each step brings you closer to your goal.

Setting milestones along the way can help keep your momentum going. Milestones act as checkpoints, allowing you to track your progress and maintain motivation. They're like little victories that keep your spirits high, even if the final goal is still far off. Identifying important milestones in your goal-setting helps you keep track of how far you've come and what's left to achieve. For example, if your goal is to learn a new language, a milestone could be holding a basic conversation or understanding a short story in that language. Celebrating these achievements, no matter how small, reinforces your progress and propels you to keep pushing forward. It's a reminder that every step, no matter how minor, counts toward your overall success.

Reflection is an often overlooked but vital part of achieving goals, but we know better. Regularly assessing your progress lets you see what's working and what might need tweaking. Weekly progress assessments can provide valuable insights into the effectiveness of how you've broken down your tasks. Are there tasks that keep getting pushed aside? Maybe they need to be broken down further or prioritized differently. Adjusting your task lists based on these reflections helps you remain on the right track. This flexibility allows you to adapt to any challenges or changes that arise, keeping you aligned with your ultimate goal. By taking the time to reflect, you gain a clearer understanding of your journey and the steps needed to reach your destination.

Visual Element: Goal Breakdown Chart

Consider creating a goal breakdown chart:

1. Start with your primary goal at the top, and then branch out into smaller tasks and milestones.
2. Visually mapping out your goal can provide clarity and help you see the path you need to take. This chart acts as a roadmap, guiding you through each step and keeping you focused on the tasks at hand.
3. Hang it somewhere visible, like above your desk, so you're constantly reminded of your progress and what lies ahead.

This visual representation reinforces the idea that every small step contributes to the bigger picture.

TRACKING PROGRESS: USING APPS AND TOOLS FOR ACCOUNTABILITY

Think of progress tracking as your personal coach, keeping you on track and cheering you on as you move toward your goals. In today's digital age, there are tons of apps and tools designed to help you stay accountable. Take Habitica, for example. It turns your goals into a role-playing game, where completing tasks earns you rewards and levels up your character. It's a fun way to stay motivated as you watch your progress unfold in a virtual world. Then there's Trello, a project management tool that lets you organize tasks on customizable boards. It's like having a digital bulletin board where you can move tasks around, set deadlines, and even collaborate with friends on group projects. These tools keep you organized while visually representing your progress, making it easier to see how far you've come.

Choosing the right tool for you is all about finding what fits your style. Start by evaluating the features of each app. Do you prefer something simple and intuitive, or are you looking for advanced features like goal-setting templates and analytics? Also, consider if it's compatible with your devices. If you're always on the go, an app that syncs across your phone, tablet, and computer might be a better fit. Remember, the best tool is one that you find easy and enjoyable to use, encouraging you to stick with it over time. It's worth trying a few different options to see which one clicks, so definitely feel free to experiment until you find your perfect match.

Tracking your progress with these tools offers several benefits that go beyond just staying organized. For starters, they give you a visual representation of your progress. Seeing tasks checked off and goals moving closer to completion can be incredibly motivating. It gives you a sense of accomplishment and reinforces the effort you've put in. These tools also encourage consistency and discipline. By setting reminders and deadlines, they help you establish routines and stick to them. You're less likely to procrastinate when you have a clear plan and can see the impact of your actions. This consistency builds momentum, making it easier to tackle challenges and stay focused on your objectives.

Like so many of the skills we're learning, regular progress reviews are an important part of this process. Schedule weekly check-ins to see how you're doing. These reviews don't have to take a long time; even a quick glance at your completed tasks can provide valuable insights. Are you moving at the pace you expected? Are there areas where you consistently fall short? Use this information to set new targets and adjust your strategies as needed. Maybe you need to make more time for a particular task or adapt your approach to make it more realistic. By regularly reviewing your progress and making necessary tweaks, you ensure you remain aligned with your goals and continue to move forward effectively.

CELEBRATING MILESTONES: THE IMPORTANCE OF REWARD

Picture this: You've just completed a challenging task, like taking a test you were dreading or finishing that art project you've been working on for weeks. How do you feel? Probably a mix of relief and pride, right? Now, imagine adding a reward to that mix—like a trip to your favorite ice cream shop or a new book you've been eyeing. Rewards are more than just treats; they're powerful motivators that reinforce positive behavior and keep you focused on your goals. By setting up incentives for reaching milestones, you boost morale and satisfaction, turning hard work into something rewarding. It's like having a personal cheerleader who motivates you to push through challenges and celebrate your successes.

It's important to choose the proper reward. It should be meaningful and line up with what you value. Start by personalizing rewards to suit you. If you love music, maybe your reward is downloading a new album or attending a concert. If you're a foodie, perhaps it's trying out a new recipe or dining at a restaurant you've been curious about. The key is to balance short-term gratification with long-term goals. While a small treat can provide immediate satisfaction, ensure it aligns with your objectives. For instance, if saving money is a goal, a reward could be putting a small amount into a fund for something bigger you're looking forward to. The reward doesn't have to be over the top; it just needs to be something that feels special and motivating to you.

When and how often you get rewards has a big influence on how effective they are. Think about immediate versus delayed rewards. Immediate rewards, like a quick snack break after completing a study session, can provide instant encouragement. On the other hand, delayed rewards, like a weekend outing after finishing a significant project, build anticipation and offer a greater sense of accomplishment.

Consider the frequency, too. Rewarding yourself too often might make it so you're not as excited, while rewards that are too infrequent might cause you to lose motivation. Find the right balance. Perhaps smaller rewards can be frequent, while larger ones are reserved for bigger milestones. This balance keeps the reward system fresh and engaging, maintaining your enthusiasm as you go after your goals.

Again, reflecting on the effectiveness of your reward system is essential for keeping your motivation strategy sharp. Regularly analyze how your rewards impact your progress. Do they boost your motivation and help you stay focused, or do they sometimes feel like an afterthought? Adjust your reward system based on your answers. If you notice that some rewards aren't as motivating as you expected, tweak them to better fit your circumstances. Maybe you're interested in a new hobby, and incorporating it into your reward system could renew your enthusiasm. By staying flexible and attentive to what truly excites you, you ensure that your rewards remain relevant and inspiring, propelling you toward your goals with renewed excitement.

STAYING FLEXIBLE: ADJUSTING GOALS AS YOU GROW

Imagine you're on a road trip with your family, and suddenly, there's a detour sign forcing you to find a new route. At first, it might seem inconvenient, but often, these detours lead to unexpected discoveries and new adventures. Similarly, in life, flexibility in your goals is like that detour sign. Being flexible means you can adapt to the twists and turns that come your way. Maintaining flexibility means being open to change and uncertainty, which is a natural part of life. Your values and priorities might shift as you grow, and your goals should align with these changing aspects of who you are. Embracing flexibility allows you to adjust your path without feeling like you're losing direction.

Regularly reassess and adjust your goals to reflect your growth and development. Think of it as a routine check-up but for your ambitions. Set aside time to evaluate your goals, considering whether they still align with where you want to head. Are they still relevant to your current life situation? This evaluation process involves self-reflection, where you take a step back and assess what's working and what's not. It's also about implementing changes based on this reflection. Maybe you've realized that a particular goal no longer excites you or that your interests have shifted. Adjusting your goals based on these insights ensures they remain meaningful and motivating. It's like tuning an instrument to ensure it plays harmoniously with the rest of the orchestra.

This is another area where adopting a growth mindset is vital to viewing adjustments not as failures but as opportunities for learning and improvement. This mindset encourages you to embrace challenges as valuable learning experiences. Instead of seeing setbacks as roadblocks, view them as stepping stones that guide you to new opportunities. Each challenge is a chance to grow stronger and wiser. With a growth mindset, you understand that change is not something to fear but something to welcome. It's about being open to new possibilities and seeing adjustments as part of your personal self-improvement journey. This perspective makes you more resilient and empowers you to navigate life with confidence.

Think about stories of individuals who have successfully adapted their goals to changing circumstances. Take the athlete who, after an unexpected injury, had to adjust their training goals. Instead of giving up, they focused on rehabilitation and exploring new strengths, ultimately returning stronger than before. Or think of the student who realized their passion lay in a different field and changed their academic goals accordingly. By embracing their newfound interests, they were able to pursue a path that truly spoke to them. These stories highlight the importance of being adaptable and open to change. They remind us that it's okay to shift directions when our circumstances or passions evolve and that doing so can lead to unexpected achievements.

In the bigger picture, staying flexible in your goals connects to the broader theme of self-discovery and growth. It's about recognizing that change is a constant in life and that adapting to it helps you thrive. As you continue on your path, remember that it's perfectly fine to adjust your goals to fit your current reality. This ensures that your goals remain relevant and empowers you to pursue them with renewed enthusiasm. Embrace the idea that your goals are not set in stone but are dynamic and capable of evolving along with you. This flexibility is what keeps your journey exciting and full of potential!

8

BUILDING INDEPENDENCE AND STEPPING INTO ADULTHOOD

For this last chapter, I want you to imagine you're at the edge of a beautiful waterfall, ready to dive in. The water below is deep and a little intimidating, but the idea of jumping in is exciting, too. That's what it feels like stepping into adulthood. Independence becomes more than just a word thrown around by parents and teachers; it's a reality you're preparing to face. Building independence involves mastering essential skills, much like learning the perfect dive. These skills aren't simply about surviving; they're about thriving in both personal and professional settings. Let's dive into the waters of adulting and see how you can swim confidently through life's challenges.

EMBRACING ADULTING: DEVELOPING SKILLS FOR INDEPENDENCE

When it comes to adulting, there's a toolkit of skills every teen should have. Budgeting and financial literacy are at the top of the list. Imagine knowing exactly how much you can spend on that new game or saving up for a big concert without running out of cash. Budgeting is all about understanding how much you make and your expenses so you are not caught off guard. Let's take a closer look at what you need in your adulting toolkit:

As far as budgeting goes, start by tracking how much money you spend each day. Apps like Mint or even a simple spreadsheet can help you keep tabs on where your money goes. This habit keeps your finances in check and helps you make smart decisions about your spending.

Next up is basic cooking and meal planning. Whether you're heading to college or planning your first solo trip, knowing how to whip up a healthy meal is important. Start with simple recipes like pasta or scrambled eggs and gradually advance to more complex dishes as you gain confidence. Meal planning is equally essential. It's about deciding what you'll eat for the week, making grocery lists, and sticking to them. This saves time and money and ensures you're eating a balanced diet. Plus, cooking at home can be a fun, creative outlet and a great way to impress friends and family with your culinary skills.

The time management skills we've talked about are another cornerstone of independence. Balancing school, work, and leisure requires a well-organized schedule. It's about prioritizing tasks and commitments and making sure you have time for responsibilities and relaxation. You can revisit Chapter 2 for a refresher on the time management skills we learned. But something as simple as a planner or digital calendar can be your best friend here, helping you visualize your time and avoid the dreaded last-minute rush. By mastering time management, you're setting yourself up for success in all areas of life, from managing a busy school week to tackling a demanding job.

Building these skills will benefit you in a lot of ways. First, there's increased self-reliance. Knowing you can handle tasks on your own boosts your confidence and reduces the anxiety of facing new challenges. It's about being prepared and capable, whether you're handling a minor crisis or making everyday decisions. These skills also enhance your problem-solving abilities. Life throws curveballs, and having the skills to navigate them makes all the difference. Whether it's fixing a small issue at home or resolving a conflict at work, being resourceful and adaptable ensures you can handle whatever comes your way.

Getting some real-world experience can go a long way. Consider taking a part-time job or volunteering in community service projects. These opportunities provide experience where you can apply budgeting, time management, and other skills. A part-time job not only brings in extra cash but also teaches you responsibility, teamwork, and effective communication. Volunteering is an opportunity to give back while you develop empathy and leadership skills. Both paths give you the experience you need to transition smoothly into adulthood, making you more adaptable and resilient in the face of new challenges.

Interactive Element: Budgeting Challenge

Try this budgeting challenge:

Set a weekly allowance for yourself and stick to it.

1. Track every expense—coffee, snacks, movie tickets—and see where your money goes.
2. At the end of the week, review your spending.
3. Did you overspend in some areas? Could you save more?

This exercise enhances your budgeting skills and provides insight into your spending habits. Adjust your budget for the following week based on what you learn.

HARNESSING TECHNOLOGY WISELY: BALANCING USE AND AVOIDING PITFALLS

In today's digital age, technology is like a double-edged sword. On one side, it can be an incredible tool for independence, helping you organize your life and stay productive. On the other, it can quickly become a distraction, pulling you into endless scrolling and mindless clicking. Digital tools are excellent for organization. Apps like Google Keep or Notion let you jot down ideas, create to-do lists, and set reminders. They're like having a personal assistant in your pocket, ensuring you don't forget about that essay due next week. However, it's easy to fall into the trap of digital distractions. Notifications pinging every few minutes can break your concentration and lead to procrastination. Overuse can also lead to one of those nights where you realize you've spent hours watching videos instead of studying.

The key is finding a balance that lets you maximize the benefits of technology and minimize the drawbacks. Start by setting screen time limits. Your phone or tablet likely has settings that allow you to monitor and limit your usage. Decide how much time you want to spend on social media or gaming each day, and stick to it. This helps keep your digital life in check and frees up time for offline activities. Speaking of which, prioritize those offline moments. Read a book, play a musical instrument, or go for a walk outside. These activities give your eyes a break from screens and boost your creativity and physical health.

You need to develop digital literacy to use technology responsibly. The first step is to understand online privacy and security. Be aware of what information you're sharing and with whom. Use strong, unique passwords for different accounts, and consider two-factor authentication for added security. It's also important to evaluate the credibility of online information. There is endless content out there, and not everything you read is true. Learn to spot reliable sources, check the facts, and think critically about the information you consume. This skill is like a shield against misinformation, ensuring you're well-informed and capable of making good decisions.

Being a responsible digital citizen means more than protecting your data; it's about how you interact online. Engage positively on social media by sharing uplifting content, supporting friends, and joining constructive discussions. Remember, the things you post can have a lasting impact, not just on others, but on your own digital footprint. It's also about respecting others' digital boundaries. Not everyone wants their photo shared or their messages posted publicly. Always ask permission before posting about someone else, and respect their decision if they say no. This respect builds trust and healthy online relationships, making the digital world a more positive place for everyone.

Interactive Element: Digital Balance Exercise

Try this digital balance exercise:

1. For one week, track your screen time and note how you feel after each session.
2. Are there specific apps that leave you feeling drained or anxious?
3. At the end of the week, reflect on your findings and make adjustments.
4. Consider removing apps that don't add value to your life or setting stricter time limits.

This exercise will help you become more mindful of your technology use and encourage a healthier balance between online and offline activities.

Peer Networking: Building a Supportive Squad

Think about your favorite movie or TV show. The hero always has a squad—a group of friends who are there through thick and thin, offering support, sharing ideas, and cheering each other on. That's what a strong peer network is like in real life, and it's a game-changer for your personal and academic growth. Imagine having friends who share resources, whether it's notes for a class or advice on handling a tricky situation. They provide emotional support and encouragement, turning difficult days into manageable ones. In times of stress, having someone to talk to can be comforting, and knowing that you're not alone makes a huge difference.

Building and maintaining these connections takes effort, but it's worth it. Start by joining clubs and groups at school or in your community. Whether it's a book club, a sports team, or a robotics group, these settings are perfect for meeting people who share your passions. Participating in team-based projects also creates strong connections. Working toward a common goal builds camaraderie and helps you learn from each other's strengths. These activities create opportunities to bond over shared experiences, forming friendships that can last a lifetime. It's about creating a network of people who have your back, just like you have theirs.

The beauty of a diverse network is the variety of perspectives it brings. When your squad includes people from different backgrounds and cultures, you get to learn new ideas and ways of thinking. This diversity enriches your understanding of the world, challenging your assumptions and broadening your horizons. Learning with others becomes a thrilling adventure when you approach problems from multiple angles. Each person brings unique insights, sparking creativity and innovation. This environment encourages you to think critically and adapt to different viewpoints. These skills are invaluable both in school and in life.

To grow your peer network, attend social events and workshops where you can meet new people. These gatherings are great for expanding your circle and discovering potential connections. Try not to be a wallflower—introduce yourself, ask questions, and show genuine interest in others. Organizing study groups or peer mentoring sessions is another great way to strengthen your network. Study groups help with academics while also building a sense of community. You learn together, celebrate successes, and support each other through challenges. You can also get involved in peer mentoring and share your wisdom and experiences with others.

Interactive Element: Networking Challenge

Try this networking challenge:

1. Attend a club meeting or community event you're interested in but haven't yet explored.
2. Take a friend if it helps ease nerves, but make a conscious effort to meet at least one new person.
3. Follow up with them later, perhaps by sharing a resource or inviting them to join a study session.
4. Reflect on how expanding your network impacts your perspective and opportunities.

By building a supportive peer network, you create a solid foundation for personal and academic growth. These connections offer more than just friendship—they provide a support system that helps you navigate life with confidence and resilience. Each interaction is an opportunity to learn, grow, and contribute to a community of like-minded individuals. As you develop these relationships, you'll find yourself more prepared to face challenges and seize opportunities.

LEARNING TO ASK FOR HELP: BUILDING A NETWORK OF SUPPORT

Picture this: You're sitting at your desk, staring at a math problem that looks like it's written in a foreign language. You've tried every angle, but the solution seems just out of reach. It's tempting to power through alone, fearing that asking for help might make you seem less capable. But here's the truth: Seeking help is actually a strength, not a weakness. When you reach out, you gain access to valuable insights and new perspectives that you might not have considered. Think of it as a way to pull in some fresh air when you're stuck in a stuffy room. This not only helps you solve the problem at hand but also strengthens your relationships. When you collaborate, you build trust and create bonds that can last a lifetime.

It's important to find the right people to ask for help. Start by looking at the support networks you already have. Family members can be a great place to go, whether it's an older sibling who's already faced the challenges you're dealing with or a parent who's always ready to listen. Mentors are a good source of help, too. They offer guidance based on their experiences and can provide advice for your unique situation. Don't overlook teachers and counselors, either. They have a wealth of knowledge and are often eager to help you succeed. It might feel intimidating at first, but remember, these people are in your corner and want to see you succeed.

Knowing how to communicate your needs effectively is key to getting the support you need, so make sure to lean on the communication skills you've learned. Start by stating your needs clearly. Instead of saying, "I don't get it," try, "I'm struggling with this part of the problem." This direct approach helps others understand precisely where you need help. Practice active listening when they respond. This means really focusing on what they're saying, nodding to show you're engaged, and asking follow-up questions if needed. Active listening isn't just about hearing words; it's about understanding the message. This back-and-forth exchange clarifies your understanding and shows respect for the person helping you, strengthening your connection with them.

As you build a supportive network, make sure that your relationships go both ways. When someone helps you, offer your assistance in return. Maybe a classmate helped you with that tricky math problem; next time, you could help them with their English essay. This mutual exchange builds a foundation of trust and cooperation, ensuring that support is always a two-way street. Keep communication lines open, even when you don't need immediate help. Check in with your network regularly, ask how they're doing, and offer support when you can. This steady communication strengthens relationships and ensures that when you need help, it feels natural and comfortable to ask for it.

Interactive Element: Support Network Mapping

Try this exercise:

1. Create a map of your support network.
2. Start by writing your name in the center of a piece of paper.
3. Then, around it, list family members, friends, mentors, teachers, or anyone you can turn to for help.
4. Draw lines connecting you to each person and note the type of support they offer (emotional, academic, etc.).
5. Reflect on areas where your network is strong and where you might want to expand it.

This visual representation can help you see the support you have and identify any gaps, encouraging you to reach out and strengthen those connections.

CREATING A PERSONAL GROWTH PLAN: MAPPING YOUR FUTURE

Now, imagine you're a captain setting sail on an open sea. To avoid drifting aimlessly, you'll need a map—a personal growth plan. This isn't just about setting goals; it's about defining your values and aspirations, the things that matter most to you. It's like plotting your course toward the horizon, where your dreams and ambitions lie. Start by thinking about what truly excites you, what you're passionate about, and where you see yourself in the future. These are what are called your core values, and they are like your compass, guiding your decisions and actions. Once you've identified these core values, it's time to map steps to turn these dreams into reality. Breaking down long-term goals into smaller, achievable steps makes them less daunting and much more real. Each step is like a milestone, a checkmark on your map signaling that you're moving in the right direction.

To build your growth plan, begin with a self-assessment. This involves taking an honest look at your strengths and weaknesses. Knowing what you're good at and where you struggle helps you craft a plan that plays to your strengths while addressing areas for improvement. It's like knowing the capabilities of your ship before setting sail. Next, set short-term and long-term objectives. Short-term goals are the stepping stones—like learning a new skill or improving grades—while long-term goals might include career goals or personal achievements. Write these goals down, making them specific and time-bound, like we learned when we discussed setting SMART goals. This process transforms abstract dreams into concrete targets, setting the stage for real progress.

A personal growth plan offers more than just direction. It provides motivation and a sense of purpose. Knowing why you're doing something makes it easier to persevere through challenges. This plan also increases your self-awareness, helping you understand your priorities and align your actions with your values. It's like having a north star that keeps you focused and accountable, reminding you of what's truly important. Plus, as you achieve each goal, your confidence grows, reinforcing the belief that you can reach even higher.

Take time to regularly review and adjust your growth plan. Life is constantly changing, and so are your goals and circumstances. Every few months, schedule self-reflection sessions to assess your progress and ensure that your plan is still relevant. During these sessions, ask yourself what's working, what's not, and why. Are your goals still aligned with your values, or do they need tweaking? This reflection is like recalibrating your compass, ensuring you're still heading toward your destination. Update your goals and action steps as needed, embracing the changes that life brings. This adaptability is critical to staying on course, even when the seas are rough.

To stay engaged with your growth plan, incorporate visual elements. Create a vision board with images and words that represent your goals. It's a creative way to visualize your future and stay inspired.

Hang it somewhere visible as a daily reminder of where you're headed. As you achieve each goal, celebrate your progress. Recognize the hard work and dedication it took to get there, and use that momentum to propel you forward. This celebration isn't just about the destination; it's about acknowledging the journey and the growth you've experienced along the way.

Visual Element: Vision Board Challenge

Make your own vision board to help you stay on track with your goals:

Gather magazines, printouts, or digital images that resonate with your goals and aspirations.

1. Create a collage on a poster board or digital platform.
2. Arrange them in a way that tells the story of your future.
3. Place your vision board where you'll see it daily.
4. Reflect on it regularly and update it as your goals evolve.

This exercise reinforces your goals and keeps your motivation alive and vibrant.

CELEBRATING YOUR JOURNEY: REFLECTING ON GROWTH AND PLANNING AHEAD

Think back to the last time you reached a goal. The sense of accomplishment, that feeling of pride—it's like finally beating a difficult level in a game. But how often do you take the time to truly reflect on your achievements? Reflection isn't just a pat on the back; it's a chance to understand your journey, recognize your progress, and gain insights from past experiences. It's about acknowledging how far you've come and pinpointing what got you there. By regularly reflecting on your growth, you create a clearer picture of what works and what doesn't, setting yourself up for even greater success in the future.

Along those same lines, celebrating milestones isn't just about throwing a party—though that can be fun, too! It's about marking the moments that matter and recognizing your hard work. Maybe you've aced a big test, learned a new skill, or completed a significant project. A small gathering with friends and family is a great way to share your success and feel supported. It doesn't have to be complicated; a simple pizza night or a picnic in the park can be just as meaningful. You could also keep a personal journal to remind yourself of your accomplishments. Write down what you did, how you felt, and why it mattered. This personal record becomes a source of motivation during tougher times, reminding you that you've overcome challenges before and can do it again.

As with all the skills we've talked about, it's essential to reflect as you plan your future growth. By looking back, you can find areas for improvement and set new, challenging goals. Ask yourself: What did I learn from this experience? What could I have done differently? These questions help you fine-tune your approach, making your future efforts more effective. It's about learning from both your successes and your mistakes. You can understand what fueled your achievements and what might have held you back. This reflective practice isn't just about fixing what went wrong; it's about building on what went right, ensuring each step you take is more confident and purposeful.

Having a forward-thinking mindset helps you grow. It means staying open to new opportunities, even when you feel uncertain. Embrace change as a chance to learn and develop rather than something to fear. Life's unpredictability can be daunting, but it's also where the most exciting opportunities lie. Seeking continuous learning and development keeps your skills sharp and your mind quick. Whether it's taking up a new hobby, enrolling in a class, or simply reading more, staying curious and engaged ensures you're continually growing. It's about looking ahead excitedly, exploring new paths, and embracing the unknown.

Reflecting on your journey and celebrating your milestones builds a strong foundation for personal growth. It's about recognizing where you've been and using that knowledge to guide where you're going. As you continue to develop your independence and learn to rely on yourself, these practices will help you navigate the challenges and opportunities ahead. Your journey doesn't end here; it's just beginning. Keep pushing forward, stay open to new experiences, and remember to celebrate your achievements along the way. Each step you take brings you closer to becoming the person you aspire to be, equipped with the skills and mindset to thrive in every aspect of life.

CONCLUSION

Congratulations on reaching the end of this book! You've taken big steps toward understanding and mastering executive functioning skills. We've journeyed together through a range of topics, from breaking down the basics of executive functioning to applying these skills in everyday life. Whether it was about organizing your schoolwork, managing your time, or making informed decisions, each chapter equipped you with tools for success. You've learned that executive functioning is like your brain's personal assistant, helping you navigate both school challenges and life's unpredictable moments.

The purpose of this book is to empower you to reduce stress and unlock your potential. I want to inspire you to take control of your personal development, not just in school but in every aspect of your life. My vision is for you to feel motivated and excited about the possibilities that lie ahead.

Each chapter presented key takeaways. You learned the importance of time management and how to make a schedule that works for you. We explored how to overcome procrastination and build strong organizational habits. You discovered techniques for emotional regulation and resilience, which are essential for staying calm under pressure and bouncing back from setbacks. We also delved into decision-making skills, setting and achieving SMART goals, and building independence. These skills are not just for now—they will serve you well into adulthood.

Now, let's take a moment for self-reflection. Think about how your understanding of executive functioning has grown. How have you applied these skills in your daily life? Maybe you've noticed improvements in your ability to focus on tasks, manage stress, or organize your space. Reflect on these changes and celebrate how far you've come. Self-awareness is a powerful tool in your journey of personal growth.

As you move forward, I encourage you to implement the strategies you've learned. Set specific, measurable goals for improving your executive functioning skills. Regularly assess your progress and be open to adjusting your approach as needed. Remember, personal development is an ongoing journey. Stay committed to exploring new techniques and adapting your strategies as you grow. Embrace challenges as opportunities for growth and continue to build resilience.

It's important to celebrate your achievements along the way. Recognize the small victories and the big ones, too. Each step forward is a testament to your hard work and determination. Celebrating progress boosts your motivation and reinforces those positive habits, making it easier to stay on track.

Thank you for joining me on this journey. Your commitment to self-improvement is inspiring, and I hope this book has provided valuable insights and tools for your personal and academic success. It's been a privilege to share this journey with you!

If you want to continue learning, join my readers list by scanning the QR code below. You'll gain access to an exclusive group for my readers, where you can connect with others on a similar path. You'll also get early access to new books, be notified when I offer existing books

CONCLUSION | 113

for free on Amazon, and discover fun content, including videos. It's a great way to stay engaged and continue your growth journey.

Thank you for being a part of this adventure. Remember, you have the skills and potential to achieve great things. Keep pushing forward, stay curious, and never stop learning. Your future is bright, and I can't wait to see your accomplishments!

bit.ly/FreeBooks4Teens

REFERENCES

Ackerman, C. (2017, December 21). *8 Powerful Self-Compassion Exercises & Worksheets.* Positive Psychology. https://positivepsychology.com/self-compassion-exercises-worksheets/

Ackerman, C. (2019, April 28). *42 Goal Setting Activities for Students & Kids (+ PDF).* Positive Psychology. https://positivepsychology.com/goal-setting-students-kids/

Adolescent Neurodevelopment. (2014, April 10). PubMed. https://pmc.ncbi.nlm.nih.gov/articles/PMC3982854/

Barkley, R. A. (2012). *Executive Functions: What They Are, How They Work, and Why They Evolved.* Guilford Press.

The Benefits of Flexible Goal Setting. (n.d.). Wellbeing People. https://wellbeingpeople.com/workplace-wellbeing/the-benefits-of-flexible-goal-setting/2023/#:~

Brieant, A., King-Casas, B., & Kim-Spoon, J. (2022). Predictors of Executive Function Trajectories in Adolescents With and Without ADHD: Links With Academic Outcomes. *Journal of Clinical Child and Adolescent Psychology, 51*(5), 697-710.

Building Resilience in Children and Teens. (2023, January 3). Newport Academy. https://www.newportacademy.com/resources/well-being/resilience-in-teens/

Cantrell, S. C., Almasi, J. F., Carter, J. S., Rintamaa, M., & Madden, A. (2010). The Impact of a Strategy-Based Intervention on Comprehension and Strategy Use of Struggling Adolescent Readers. *Journal of Educational Psychology, 102*(2), 257–280. https://doi.org/10.1037/a0018212

Center on the Developing Child at Harvard University. (2011). *Building the Brain's "Air Traffic Control" System: How Early Experiences Shape the Development of Executive Function.* Center on the Developing Child. https://developingchild.harvard.edu

Center on the Developing Child at Harvard University. (2016). *Executive Function and Self-Regulation: An Emerging Science* (Working Paper No. 11). Center on the Developing Child. https://developingchild.harvard.edu

Center on the Developing Child at Harvard University. (2017). *The Science of Early Childhood Development: Closing the Gap Between What We Know and What We Do.* Center on the Developing Child. https://developingchild.harvard.edu

Cognitive Restructuring to Manage Procrastination. (n.d.). Specialty Behavioral Health. https://specialtybehavioralhealth.com/cognitive-approach-to-overcoming-procrastination/

Cookson, D. (2024, March 24). *The Benefits and Drawbacks of Intuitive Thinking.* Greater Good Magazine. https://greatergood.berkeley.edu/article/item/the_benefits_and_drawbacks_of_intuitive_thinking

Davidson, M. C., Amso, D., Anderson, L. C., & Diamond, A. (2006). Development of Cognitive Control and Executive Functions From 4 to 13 years: Evidence From

116 | REFERENCES

Manipulations of Memory, Inhibition, and Task Switching. *Neuropsychologia, 44*(11), 2037–2078. https://doi.org/10.1016/j.neuropsychologia.2006.02.006

Diamond, A. (2013). Executive functions. *Annual Review of Psychology, 64*, 135-168. https://doi.org/10.1146/annurev-psych-113011-143750

Dienlin, T. & Johannes, N. (2020, June 22). *The Impact of Digital Technology Use on Adolescent Well-Being.* PubMed. https://pmc.ncbi.nlm.nih.gov/articles/PMC7366938/

Discover 10 Best Goal-Setting Apps for Students in 2024! (2024, May 9). Amberblog. https://amberstudent.com/blog/post/best-goal-setting-apps

8 Tips on How to Help a Teen Regulate Their Emotions. (2024, February 4). Lilac Center. https://www.lilaccenter.org/blog/8-tips-on-how-to-help-a-teen-regulate-their-emotions

Executive Functions (2014, July 7). PubMed. https://pmc.ncbi.nlm.nih.gov/articles/PMC4084861/

5 Tips for Color-Coding Your Notes. (n.d.). Study.com. https://study.com/blog/5-tips-for-color-coding-your-notes.html

Fostering Personal Growth in Teenagers: Strategies for Nurturing Self-Development. (n.d.). The Attitude Advantage. https://theattitudeadvantage.com/all-posts/fostering-personal-growth-in-teenagers-strategies-for-nurturing-self-development/

Friedman, N. P., Miyake, A., Young, S. E., DeFries, J. C., Corley, R. P., & Hewitt, J. K. (2008). Individual Differences in Executive Functions Are Almost Entirely Genetic in Origin. *Journal of Clinical Child and Adolescent Psychology, 37*(4), 674-685.

Gladson, N. (2024, January 29). *How to Inspire Student Goals With Vision Boards.* Connections Academy. Goal-Setting

A Guide to Enhancing Decision-Making Skills All Posts. (n.d.). The Attitude Advantage. https://theattitudeadvantage.com/all-posts/empowering-teens-to-make-smart-choices-a-guide-to-enhancing-decision-making-skills/

Hanson, C. (2024, September 2). *How To Use The Eisenhower Matrix To Help Your Teen Plan Their Day.* Life Skills Advocate. https://lifeskillsadvocate.com/blog/eisenhower-matrix/

Ingram, S. (2024, September 30). *35 Essential Life Skills For Teens To Master By Age 18.* Rustic Pathways. https://rusticpathways.com/inside-rustic/online-magazine/11-life-skills-every-teen-should-have-by-age-18

Jensen, F. E., & Nutt, A. E. (2015). *The Teenage Brain: A Neuroscientist's Survival Guide to Raising Adolescents and Young Adults.* Harper.

J. R., & Miller, P. H. (2010). A Developmental Perspective on Executive Function. *Child Development, 81*(6), 1641–1660. https://doi.org/10.1111/j.1467-8624.2010.01499.x

The Journal of Neuroscience. (2013). *Functional Maturation of the Executive System During Adolescence. The Journal of Neuroscience, 33*(41), 16202–16212.

The Journal of Neuroscience. (2022). *Changes in Behavior and Neural Dynamics Across Adolescent Development. The Journal of Neuroscience, 42*(8), 1520–1536.

The Journal of Neuroscience. (2010). *Executive Function, Maturation, and Cognitive Control. The Journal of Neuroscience, 30*(32), 10980–10992.

KidsHealth Medical Experts. (n.d.). *Confidence (for Teens).* Nemours TeensHealth. https://kidshealth.org/en/teens/confidence.html

REFERENCES | 117

Makohon, A. (2023, October 6). *Best 8 meditation and mindfulness apps for teens.* Treblab. https://treblab.com/blogs/news/best-meditation-apps-for-teens

National Institute of Mental Health. (n.d.). *Mental Health Minute: Stress and Anxiety in Adolescents.* National Institute of Mental Health. https://www.nimh.nih.gov

National Institute of Mental Health. (n.d.). *Adolescent Brain Cognitive Development (ABCD) study.* National Institute of Mental Health. https://www.nimh.nih.gov

National Institute of Mental Health. (n.d.). *Resources for students and educators.* National Institute of Mental Health. https://www.nimh.nih.gov

Note-Taking Apps for Tweens and Teens. (n.d.). Common Sense Media. https://www.commonsensemedia.org/lists/note-taking-apps-for-tweens-and-teens

Nyongesa, M. K., Ssewanyana, D., Mutua, A. M., Chongwo, E., Scerif, G., Newton, C. R., & Abubakar, A. (2019). Assessing Executive Function in Adolescence: A Scoping Review of Existing Measures and Their Psychometric Robustness. *Journal of Clinical Child and Adolescent Psychology, 48*(6), 927-943.

Pediatrics. (2024, April 22). *How Does Peer Pressure Affect a Teen's Social Development?* Scripps. https://www.scripps.org/news_items/4648-how-does-peer-pressure-affect-a-teen-s-social-development#:~

Plan and Connect With Microsoft To Do. (n.d.). Microsoft. https://support.microsoft.com/en-us/office/plan-and-connect-with-microsoft-to-do-f64171ef-f550-4151-bae3-492720f3f1aa

The Psychology of Procrastination in Teens. (n.d.). Pacific Coast Therapy. https://pacificcoasttherapy.com/the-psychology-of-procrastination-in-teens/

Rad, H. et al. (2023, January) *Mindfulness Intervention for Academic Procrastination: A Randomized Control Trial.* Science Direct. https://www.sciencedirect.com/science/article/abs/pii/S1041608022001315

Richard. (2023, December 19). *Teenage Time Management Apps: 5 Best Picks for Focus & Efficiency.* Teen Coach Academy. https://teencoachacademy.com/blog/teenage-time-management-apps/

Siegel, D. J. (2012). *The Developing Mind: How Relationships and the Brain Interact to Shape Who We Are* (2nd ed.). Guilford Press.

SMART Goals for Teens. (n.d.). Your Therapy Source. https://www.yourtherapysource.com/blog1/2022/08/11/smart-goals-for-teens-3/

Teens Can Improve Focus with the Pomodoro Technique. (n.d.). Blue Stars Admissions Consulting. https://bluestars.us/teens-can-improve-focus-with-the-pomodoro-technique/#:~:text=In%20short%2C%20the%20Pomodoro%20Technique

Tome, G. et al. (2012, March 1). *How Can Peer Group Influence the Behavior of Adolescents?* PubMed. https://pmc.ncbi.nlm.nih.gov/articles/PMC4777050/

12 Tips to Balance Academics and Extracurricular Activities. (n.d.). The Princeton Review. https://www.princetonreview.com/college-advice/12-tips-to-balance-academics-and-extracurriculars

20 Tips to Motivate Your Teen to Declutter Their Room (by a Teen). (n.d.). The Simplicity Habit. https://www.thesimplicityhabit.com/motivate-your-teen-to-declutter/

Zimmerman, B. J., & Schunk, D. H. (Eds.). (2011). *Handbook of Self-regulation of Learning and Performance.* Routledge.

REFERENCES

Underwood, E. (2023, April 20). *Teens can have excellent executive function — just not all the time.* Knowable. https://knowablemagazine.org/content/article/mind/2023/executive-function-in-teen-brains

Made in United States
Orlando, FL
04 May 2025